MW01481885

Wreck Beach

Published by New Star Books

Series Editor: Terry Glavin

Other books in the Transmontanus series

Wreck Beach

CARELLIN BROOKS

TRANSMONTANUS ┃ NEW STAR BOOKS VANCOUVER

Wreck Beach at twilight as seen from the Oasis, the area's only natural beach. JAMES LOEWEN PHOTO

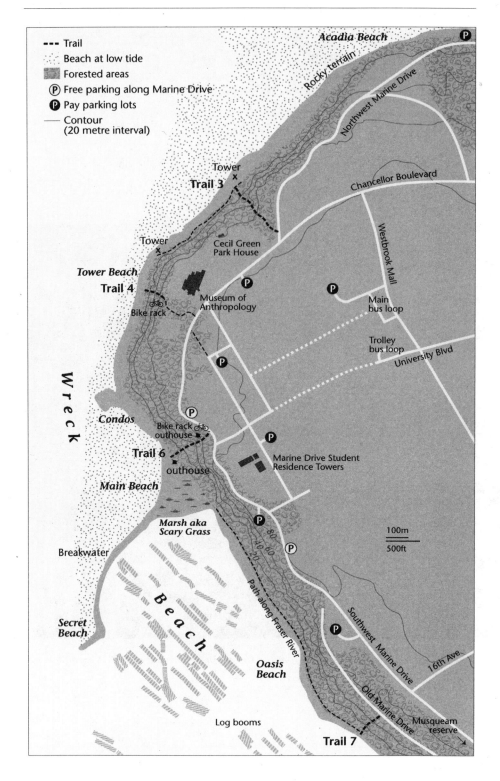

Legend:

- - - Trail
- ⠂⠂⠂ Beach at low tide
- ▨ Forested areas
- Ⓟ Free parking along Marine Drive
- 🅿 Pay parking lots
- — Contour (20 metre interval)

Acadia Beach

Rocky terrain

Northwest Marine Drive

Chancellor Boulevard

Westbrook Mall

Tower
×
Trail 3

Tower
×

Cecil Green
Park House

Tower Beach
Trail 4

Bike rack

Museum of
Anthropology

Main
bus loop

Trolley
bus loop

University Blvd

W
r
e
c
k

Condos

Bike rack
outhouse
Trail 6

outhouse

Main Beach

Marsh aka
Scary Grass

Breakwater

Marine Drive Student
Residence Towers

80
60
40
20

100m
500ft

Secret
Beach

B
e
a
c
h

Southwest Marine Drive

16th Ave.

Oasis
Beach

Old Marine Drive

Musqueam
reserve

Log booms

Path along Fraser River

Trail 7

ONE

The Beach Today

The most beautiful city in the world has two seasons: August and otherwise. Otherwise means dark and windy days and nights. In the daytime you shiver and reach for sweaters, cups of tea, thick books. At night you wonder whether it's actually necessary to go out, or if you can get away with skipping that dinner party, club gig, or late shift. There are days and days on end of penetrating drizzle; occasionally, for variety, a sudden deluge of Biblical proportions. Every so often the sun shows itself: a girl on a stage, up in the sky, crossing and recrossing her golden legs.

August is different. Each day dawns clear as an untroubled face and ends that way too. The air is rich and light, like cotton candy. As a month it's almost long enough to forget the others: October's curled leaves skittering papery along the ground, the pervading damp of November, the false hope of April, socked in with grey. Almost. But not quite.

Into this climate comes Wreck Beach, the biggest and best nude beach in Canada, possibly the world. How it got that way, how it stays that way today, and what it will become tomorrow: this is the subject of this book.

Let's go there. To get to Wreck Beach, start in midsummer — the middle of June, maybe, or July or, ideally, the best of all months, August. There are other times of year to go, certainly. There are even die-hard beachers who claim it is fine in February and November, in the right sheltered spot and with the right combination of jerry-rigged sun reflectors; but in August you will be certain of fine weather and a fine crowd. Your next decision will

Trails of Wreck Beach

Acadia Beach Trail: The northernmost trail to greater Wreck Beach is adjacent to the off-leash portion of Spanish Banks. A gentle gravelled trail, the only beach access suitable for wheelchairs and strollers, it runs from the parking lot on Marine Drive down to the beach. There is a little humpbacked wooden bridge to navigate before you come to the clothing-optional area, and some relatively rough going over the little pathlets to the beach. But the sand is hard-packed, the stones are relatively few, and, if the tide is right, there are miles of beach.

Trail Three: The trail leading down to Tower Beach is the closest to the remnants of two searchlight towers built here before the Second World War in case of Japanese attack. A military complex, Fort Point Grey, was built at the top of the cliffs and housed military personnel during the war and afterwards. By 1950, Fort Point Grey had been renamed Fort Camp. It was turned into makeshift accommodation for UBC students and demolished more than two decades later.

Trail Four: This trail is accessed from the meadow behind the Museum of Anthropology, with its longhouse, totem poles, and unfilled reflecting pool. Cecil Green Park House, while not immediately visible, is close by to your right. Also nearby is Graham's Gully, the ravine that opened on campus in 1935 after heavy rainfall. The trail offers a steep, almost breathless descent, complete with stairs and switchbacks that traverse the hill before plunging downwards again. Below is a narrow strip of sandy beach that disappears entirely at high tide. It's overhung by trees and sparsely populated by beachgoers, even at the height of summer. If you're looking for relative privacy, this is your spot.

Trail Six: The main trail to today's main beach, and the one most visitors use. Infamous for its height, its length, and the number of steps (402 by my count), it is also thoughtfully augmented with several resting spots and at least one hand-carved bench for the less-than-perfectly fit.

Trail Seven: Starting at the top of the cliff off Old Marine Drive, a good walk south of the main trail, this is the gateway to Wreck Beach's gayside, a section that differs from the main beach in geography, orientation, and even outlook. The trail is similar to Trail Six: another leafy glade, another dirt-packed trailhead, this one minus the vendors and notice boards, but displaying the official clothing-optional sign. The rushing and tinkling as you start down the steps comes from a culvert to your left, where a gush of water falls into a deep, still pool and then makes its way by degrees down the slope, here eddying, here plashing. Like all the water that courses down the cliffs, however tempting it looks, it is unsafe to drink, laced with *E. coli* and other unpleasant effluvia.

At the bottom of this trail, rustically lined with convenient, branched railings, a path stretches to left and right. There is little in the way of beach proper beyond this gladed track: the area is an estuary and a kingfisher sanctuary. Many possibilities await you here, from the beach grass of Jurassic Park at the far south end of the gay section, to the relatively manicured and spacious Oasis, which is the only real stretch of beach on gay Wreck Beach. More about these in Chapter Two.

be easy: weekday or weekend? On a weekday you can count on a relatively relaxed atmosphere, a certain sparseness. On a weekend it will all be there, the whole bag of tricks, ball of wax, three-ring circus, dog and pony show. There will be first-timers and last-timers and in-betweeners and the regulars. There will be the clothed and the unclothed and the people trying to sell them things. The police will come to keep the vendors who want to sell beer from selling it and the buyers who want to drink beer from drinking it. There will be music and muttered complaints. Kayaks will be pulled up on the rocks; Jet Skis will be roaring out in the bay; bigger boats will be anchored midway to the shore, ignoring the red bobbing buoys that demarcate the swimming area. There will be music and marijuana and mushrooms, sun umbrellas and hats and young women in bikini bottoms. There will be skimboarders practising at the tideline, and the tideline itself, ebbing and flowing as the tides compel it. In short, everything.

You'll need to get there somehow, to Point Grey, as the peninsula at the end of the western part of the city is known. It's university land out here, and parkland. The big golf course past the Endowment Lands sign on 10th Avenue, the mansions on the hill above as you cruise up 4th or Marine Drive, the vast reaches of forested parkland rolling beyond 16th — these aren't even part of Vancouver. The Endowment Lands, on which they're built, is an electoral district, not a municipality. The city police force has no jurisdiction here; only the Royal Canadian Mounted Police do.

Keep on going. You drove, so you'll need to find parking. Along Marine Drive there are a number of spots — and more often than not an equal number of cars in them. Some of these latter are ignoring the No Parking signs at the south end of the row, but the university can be counted on to get shirty about this and, in unpredictable bursts of law enforcement, tow a large number of violators away. It's a long walk back to the bus stop on campus — about fifteen minutes — so if you've brought piles of stuff with you, best mind the signs.

There are also parkades on campus. The closest one is just past Trail Six, at Gate Six. Look for the gate numbers on posts as you come around on Marine Drive. Yes, parking there costs the earth — $1.50 per half hour at the time of writing, the same as any meters you may locate on campus. (There is an all-day parking lot on campus, which is substantially cheaper at $4.25 for the day, but it's farther away than the bus loop.)

You can also use one of the two parking lots off Marine Drive maintained by the Greater Vancouver Regional District (GVRD), which controls the entire beach from the end of Spanish Banks, on the north side of the peninsula, to the Musqueam Indian reserve on the other side. The GVRD lots are tiny, however, and fill up fast. A free lot is located just past Spanish Banks, as Marine Drive begins its climb. Another lot ($5 a day) is between Trails Six and Seven. Both are on the beach side of the road.

A bit of trivia: In the middle of the 20th century this second parking lot, known as Fraserview, was the site of a seasonal restaurant called the Dolphins that served luncheons and afternoon teas on its lawns.

If you can, leave the car behind and take the bus. Anything heading for the University of British Columbia (UBC) will do, from the 99 B-Line on Broadway (and its slower cousin, the regular number 9) to the lickety-split 44 from downtown. UBC, and hence the beach, is easily accessible from almost anywhere: West Vancouver, Richmond, the Joyce Skytrain station, or any of the main avenues running east-west: 4th, King Edward, 41st. Once you get to the UBC bus loop, there is a stop — Bay 15, to be exact — for shuttle C20. This will take you the rest of the way around Marine Drive. The top of Trail Six is a request stop, so speak up.

The Dolphins Restaurant

Or walk from the bus loop: it's a pleasant stroll through campus.

The easiest thing of all would be to bike. But easy is a relative term. You'll have to come alone, or with a like-equipped party, and tackle the hill. There is no way around the hill. If you come along 16th, it is short and exceedingly sharp, reaching its summit just before Alma so you can settle into a relatively easy glide to the south part of campus. This ride will fetch you up very close to Trail Seven.

You could take 10th. This is the most punishing of the hills: a deceptively mild start, a steady rise, and ten blocks that go up and up and up until you are dead. Detour onto 8th, where there is some shade, at least, and a few nice little homesteads (check out ye olde thatched-roof cottage on the right, near the start of the hill) to dream about.

Only a masochist would bicycle up 4th Avenue. The hill is practically perpendicular and surrounded by mansions that seem to leer even as you collapse from heat exhaustion. If this doesn't do you in, the gently punishing up and down of the rolling highway beyond will.

Of all the routes in, Marine Drive is possibly the best. There are patches of shade, and the cooling sight of the sea; the hill is wind-

Until the 1960s a restaurant called The Dolphins served lunches and teas near the top of present-day Trail Six.
VANCOUVER ARCHIVES

ing and, while not easy, comparatively short; and if your reserves
fail, you can stop off any number of places before the top and still
get to be on a beach. Not all is clover here, however. There is no
shoulder to speak of, and the cars come up rather fast. There is
a small lip to the asphalt, and beyond this a narrow gravel track,
which cyclists are encouraged to use. Gravel grounds bicycle tires
only provisionally, as many a cyclist (myself included) has found
out to her cost. Even ignoring that problem, there is no space on
the path for safely passing any pedestrians you overtake. Until the
path becomes wider and paved behind a foot-high concrete barrier, about two-thirds of the way up, it is best to stay on the road.

Or you could come by sea. The least intrusive way is to kayak
— be prepared for about an hour's paddle from downtown Vancouver. There are also larger, motor-powered craft, mostly unwel-
come, that insist on anchoring just offshore. Some people bring
Jet Skis, about which regulars have mixed feelings. In the past few
years, a line of red buoys has been added to the swimming area
to mark it off, and although not everyone on boats respects this
boundary, beachgoers would certainly appreciate it if you did. In
any case, if you contemplate coming by water, you probably know
more about such things as tidal charts and compasses and clear-
ances than this book can tell you.

So we'll pretend you came by car or bike or bus and that you
are standing at the top of Trail Six. You would not know there is a
beach here unless you look. Despite years of loud cries by naysay-
ers that its nudity is an affront to the unaware, Wreck Beach is
not the sort of place people stumble upon. Your only clue to the
amount of activity far below is the six enormous refuse bins — the
dull green plastic kind, into which a human being could easily
disappear — parked in a six-metre dirt clearing that marks the top
of Trail Six. There are some squat metal posts beside the road,
painted a glossy green and striped with yellow paint. A vendor sells
packaged ice creams, chips, bottles of water misty with conden-
sation from the cooler. There is a board, usually festooned with
notices from the Wreck Beach Preservation Society. Sometimes
a table is set up beneath the board, laden with a petition or form
letters, weighted with rocks, for people to sign. On the lip of, or
tacked to, a second board are lost things, orphaned keys and sun-
glasses, turned in by the conscientious.

And there is a set of steps descending into a leafy glade. The steps are wide, regular, made of dirt fenced in by stout timber. As you start down them, jostled sometimes by other hurrying beach-goers carrying mats and coolers, you see that they skirt a ravine. There are trees and fallen timber and the particular dim cool of a West Coast forest on a sunny afternoon. Some people are threading their way up the ravine, past fallen logs and through the underbrush; they move confidently and are bronzed all over. You watch until they disappear up a couple of sketched paths to the top of the trail, where you've just been.

The ground here is dry, dusty, almost powder-like. After a few minutes of walking — heavily, because of the slope — you begin to feel grimy. At times the steps end abruptly and you are walking on gritty packed dirt embedded with stones. In places the steps widen to a makeshift clearing, where a carved log has been placed for anyone who needs to sit down. People must be able to make the climb as well as the descent, and after a long, hot day in the sun, a few beers perhaps, it's harder than it looks.

The steps go down and down, so you feel as if you're rushing into a kind of well, but the bottom here is filled not with the dark but with brightness. Down there is the sea, and if you've ever been here before, it's now that your heart begins to swell and lift, your steps to stumble in their urgency, as you hurry to get your first glimpse of the beach. You imagine you can hear the worry and murmur of the waves, or is that the wind soughing in the tops of the trees? First, though, you see the outhouses, on your left and with a lineup of people waiting to get in, stinking to high heaven despite the deodorizer they use. Past this clearing, past a thin strip of greenery, is a wash of sand. You can't see the sweep of the beach until you actually step off the last step, past the plastic bags that are always tied here on the rustic railing made from naked branches.

Now you are on the main part of Wreck Beach, at the base of Trail Six, for the first time. The sun is high in the sky, and the sky is a pale, faraway blue. Far off, the surf curls into the sea; farther still there are pale undulations of hills, deep and then quieter blue against the line of the horizon.

But between here and there are three kinds of things: sand, logs, and bodies.

That's not technically all there is. But it's the first thing to be

*Wreck Beach's
flat, sandy
shoreline
makes it
perfect for
sandcastles.*
DON SLADE
PHOTO

seen: sand, logs, and people resting against the logs, surrounded by the things they've brought. Bags and colourful spreads and snacks and books and hats and everything else. Some of the people are naked and some are partially clothed, bare-chested but wearing bathing suits or shorts, or with pareos loosely wrapped around their hips. A few favour sunhats and Ts with nothing on underneath. And some of them are fully dressed, in T-shirts and shorts or even office clothes: dark suit pants, white short-sleeved shirts, leather belts with gold buckles, loafers.

It takes all kinds, certainly here.

It's surprising, at first, how much everyone blends in, how nakedness is something you have to look for and consciously recognize: He's not wearing any clothes. She is. He's got on a shirt, but no pants. Are they . . . ? The categories already melting away in the sun.

There are clusters of people, couples, and a few people sitting by themselves. They sit on logs or, more frequently, lean against them, reclining. They wear shades. They lie face down or, conversely, stare out to sea with their heads propped up. They read thick paperbacks. They look like people on any beach, anywhere.

If it's your first time, you may be disappointed. You may have had a different idea of what a nude beach looks like; visions of

pulchritude, female or male according to your interests or incli-
nations, may have danced in your head. The first strange thing
about Wreck Beach, in fact, is not that it is a nude beach. It is that
it looks so much like any other beach.

Except more beautiful. The sweep of golden sand (dredged
from the bottom of the river, possibly contaminated, and certainly
not native to the area — but those are quibbles) and the shady
green forest behind, the sparkle of the ocean and, beyond, faded
blue hills receding into the distance: the landscape is impossible
to ignore. Thus it's only after you've looked around a little, assimi-
lated the setting, that you begin to see what's going on people-
wise. To notice — because it's a relatively subtle thing — the lack
of demarcation.

There is no clothed versus unclothed section. No, everybody
just mixes in as best they can, suited-up students next to jaybird
families, and the vendors wandering, uttering their calls. Wreck
is not officially designated a nude beach, by the way. Signs at the
tops of trails will tell you it's "clothing optional." What this means
is if nobody can force anyone to take their clothes off, neither can
they in turn be forced to put theirs on.

The regulars would prefer it if you did — take off your clothes,
that is. Longtime beachers like Marilyn Hogan will argue, with
an abiding sincerity, that the visitor will never be completely comfortable at Wreck Beach until she takes her clothes off. If you wait,
Marilyn says, until you feel completely comfortable — until the
shedding of those last few inches of fabric is a matter of perfect
indifference to you — then you will never do it at all.

Women like Precious Hutchinson, another regular, feel so
strongly about this issue that they have created their very own
clothes-free zones, marking them off with logs and decorating
them with a fine assortment of summer flowers in hollowed-out
driftwood containers. You step into these places — houses, they're
called — less than fully undressed at your peril.

The clothed may come to Wreck Beach in perfect safety, it's
true. No one will wrest them from their jeans or demand they
strip. But it is also true that to be clothed at Wreck Beach, whether
in the smallest of bikinis or the most voluminous of caftans, is to
engender a certain — how to put it? — suspicion.

Why, the regulars wonder, would you come here if you didn't

After a hard
day in the
sunshine,
Wreck Beach's
most famous
vendor Water-
melon relaxes
on the rocks.
DON SLADE
PHOTO

intend to take your clothes off? There are plenty of other beaches in the city, almost all, if not all of them, more easily accessed. This may be the loveliest one; certainly its devotees believe so. But Third Beach, in Stanley Park, has a similar semi-wilderness feel; the sea at Spanish Banks is as shallow for as long a stretch. Why come all the way to Wreck Beach, at the end of the peninsula, where the parking is a hassle, where the bus stops some ways away, where the hill winnows out all but the fittest cyclists, if you don't want to disrobe?

The regulars think they have an answer. They have a name for them, the guys who come down in pleated, dark blue pants and pale shirts, their suit jackets tossed over one shoulder with an unconvincing air of jauntiness. The men strapped into faded backpacks, sporting high-waisted, acid-wash jeans in the fashion of a decade or more ago. The ones wearing turbans and toting plastic bags. They're called gawkers. And the gawker, more than anyone else on Wreck Beach, is an object of universal scorn and contempt. He is easily spotted. He brings no book or sunhat or towel; he has no mat to unroll. Instead of lying down he stands, sometimes on a log for greater visibility, and scans the beach. He does this in a lofty, unconcerned manner, but the regulars aren't fooled. Sometimes he strolls the foot of the beach, looking, looking; sometimes he walks between the logs and bodies, head swivelling like a search-light on a stalk; sometimes he wears dark glasses and stares from the rocks where he is perched with his friends. And if you can't see him, that's even worse. In that case he must be concealed some-where, in the bushes behind the beach, doing even filthier things: taking illicit pictures, shooting video, masturbating.

You are not, needless to say, one of those, you congratulate yourself briefly as you ease your small square of cotton over your hips. You have no more sinister purpose in coming here than the usual: looking at naked people. Attractive ones, given the choice. It's important, of course, to figure out just who you'd have sex with, given worlds enough and time, but that's not the only reason you're looking. You might like to check out the competi-tion, or perhaps you want to set the whole penis-size question to rest. Then again, you could simply want to be naked yourself, an equally valid motive. You remember the freedom of skinny-dip-ping with your friends at the lake, in moonlight, as a teen, and the illicit swim you took in a neighbour's pool that other time. You have always liked the way being naked and in the world makes you feel: both naughty and pure. As if you have been added to and stripped away at the same time. You wonder how doing it in broad daylight, among thousands of others who have or have not exer-cised this same option, will be the same or different. Well, you're about to find out.

Practically, there are some necessary and some not-so-necessary supplies. Everyone will have to decide for herself whether to pack a bathing suit, but something to sit upon is a necessity. A towel will do, or one of those tatami mats, or a piece of cloth in a pinch. Shade is good, because the beach offers very little of it. There is undergrowth at the back of the beach, but most of it is too far away to offer any shelter unless you are going up the trail at the south side of the beach to the Oasis. A hat or an umbrella are useful things, especially after a few hours or for those visitors nudists cheerfully call "bucktails" — people naked for the first time, whose pale but-tocks show like the flash of white on a deer's hind end.

There is a musical section, acoustic preferred. You can always tote along your flute or guitar on the off chance that you are able to join a jam session, or make a little music on your own. It is pos-

sible to play Frisbee on the sands, or skimboard along the surf, so
if you wish to take part in those amusements, by all means bring
the necessary equipment. Beerball, by the way, is the beach's most
violent, indigenous, and unfettered recreation. It is played only by
men. The sole piece of equipment is a single can of beer on a pole.
There are no rules. Winner gets the beer.

You can, of course, pack everything you might want to eat or
drink — cans of soda, cut-up fruit, sandwiches, all the picnic
things — but it is possible to buy all of those things and more
besides. There are a few such items that are always available; their
vendors have set up permanent encampments at the back of the
beach, delineated with driftwood, and paid the GVRD hundreds
of dollars for vendor permits. They peddle coloured throws (as
dreadful as you'd expect); red-and-white-striped sun umbrellas;
sandwiches, french fries, hot dogs (real and ersatz), and burgers.
If you are wondering why the makers of these latter seem not to
embody the spirit of the beach, by the way, rest assured that they
are modestly aproned not by choice, but as a condition of their
FoodSafe permits.

This is only the tip of the food pyramid. The unlicensed vendors, the men and women who give the place the flavour of a
Mexican resort beach, who are always whispering or shouting or
speaking quite close to you as they stand or stride or wander on by,
have far more on offer. It is possible at times, though not always
and not predictably, to partake of the following: Chinese BBQ pork
buns, pizza slices, samosas with chutney, Jell-O shooters, Jamai-
can rum punch with mint, natural sodas, the ubiquitous Kokanee
beer, Smirnoff Ice coolers, marijuana, magic mushrooms, baked
goods with added THC, and so much more besides. No need to
take away your beer can; one of the roving band of recyclers with
the big black garbage bags will do it for you.

So you may want to leave your picnic lunch at home and pur-
chase comestibles at the beach. On the other hand, you may want
to bring a genuine picnic basket, and stemware, and have your
takeout chicken on real plates, with knives and forks and linen
napkins. You may even want to swan about, as I once saw a young,
extravagantly false-breasted person doing, holding a cocktail glass
complete with spiral straw and skewered, towering fruity garnish.
Nobody will be much bothered either way.

A vendor serves fruity drinks at Wreck Beach. DON SLADE PHOTO

People will, on the other hand, be bothered if you: start a fire (or even worse, start a fire and then smash your bottles into it, making it impracticable to cover the smoking mess with sand); tote along a boom box and play it at loud volume; let your dog run over other people's blankets and scatter sand on their belongings; bring your camera and take pictures; bring your speedboat and worry the swimmers; shout at naked old geezers, puttering at the edge of the waves, who are getting in the way of your skimboarding run; or litter. Everybody knows that littering is not allowed at Wreck Beach, that everything you bring in must, in time-honoured fashion, be taken out. Everybody is aware that one of the rationales for pushing a bulldozed road down the slope, with its inevitable aftermath of trippers, is garbage removal. Which makes the huge amount of trash ferreted from the sands on cleanup days rather, well, shocking.

You flout the rules at your own risk. If you insist on taking pictures without permission, that spanking new digital camera with the zoom function may accidentally find its way into the ocean. When asked about this phenomenon, regulars like Precious Hutchinson ascribe it to nature: "Wind." There is also, let's not forget, a no-violence rule at the beach.

Keep in mind that the one thing the Wreck Beach crowd most hates and fears is any hint of pedophilia. Do not take pictures of those adorable naked children without consulting their parents, no matter how cute you think the muddy little dickens are. There is a swift, rough justice dispensed by regulars who decide they have flushed out a suspected sexual predator. You would not want to fall victim to it or be handed over to police for further explanations at the top of the trail afterwards.

Speaking of the police, they are here, a recreational hazard. The RCMP patrol the place regularly, fully suited in their dark blue uniforms, belts heavy with equipment in the summer heat. They come around, especially on busy weekends, to take your open can of beer and pour it away, and if you put up a fuss or are otherwise obnoxious, they might arrest you to boot. You may return from the sea to find your pack searched and your beer gone. Yes, it is illegal for them to search your things with no better grounds for doing so than your presence on the beach. The knowledge is cold comfort, as pointing this out to them will probably not curtail their forays. Drinking in a public place without a permit is likewise illegal, and there is nowhere else in the city that it occurs on such a scale and so brazenly, with such numbers of sellers and buyers. The police say that people get drunk and then try to drive away, or they get heatstroke and have to be hovercrafted off the beach at great expense. They also admit that most people who drink, take drugs, or otherwise flout the rules do so with no ill effects, societal or personal, whatsoever.

Anyway. You're here. You've put out your towel, judging, to a nicety, the room to be left between the forbiddingly frowning naked woman on your right, wielding her thick wedge of paper, and the fully dressed girl students chattering at the other end of the log. "Bring me back someone cute," one of these latter instructs her friend, who's getting up, tugging at her bikini. "Not one of those cute guys with an ugly friend." Time to follow the bikini-tugger's lead and go for an amble.

You turned to the right as you walked out onto the beach, not out of any particular reasoning but because it seemed somehow less overwhelming. Over there, on the other side, is the main body of the beach. (Side is, of course, a misnomer; there's no demarcation, just the trickle of people coming out from the trail, turning left or right as inclination demands, and the little clear space left for their passage.) Now you decide to go down to the water and, you know, take a stroll. Look around a bit.

There are rocks out there, half-buried in the sand, barnacled, and people standing thigh-deep even hundreds of feet out. It's hot. Behind you the greenery leafs over the hidden slope, its depths shady with promise. A girl lolling in the water on a pink air mattress goes over with a squeal. A naked tanned couple stand close in the surf, embracing. The sand is firmly packed down here, and wet. Farther along you can see a massive tide pool, tepid in the sun. A couple of kids are squatting, building sandcastles. Two guys play Frisbee, leaping for the lazy arc of the disc. The skimboarders are far away, scrawled figures against the brightness of the sun in their dash and slide.

You turn and head towards the breakwater, but slowly. The thin, damp, intertidal zone is comfortable to bare feet, unlike the sand back of the houses, which is searingly hot. There are people stacked up right to the front line of logs: creepy-looking middle-aged guys (they also make up the majority of the walkers who pass you going the other way), couples, groups, and, set back from the front, the houses. The first house has a bunch of sketchy-looking guys playing guitars and bongo drums. A young guy sits on top of a stump, six feet up in the air.

There are a couple more log squares, a picnic shelter with a sign touting shiatsu, old guys playing cards under an umbrella in a driftwood enclosure. This must be the White House, where the longest of longtime regular visitors can be found. You spot Judy Williams, the doyenne of Wreck Beach, in a corner. She's blonde, perennially tanned, and reading a thick paperback. You've heard of her; everyone has. Williams visited the beach for the first time in 1971 when she was still a special-ed teacher. Since then, and especially since her recent retirement, protecting the beach has become her life's mission.

You could go on into one of the houses and lay down your mat. Nobody would stop you — unless you happened to be dressed. Then you'd have to run the gauntlet of Precious Hutchinson and her Excuse-o-Matic. Hutchinson is a regular who has compiled a list of reasons people give for not taking off their clothes. The "Handy Textile Excuse-O-Matic" lists such non-sequiturs as "I'm

Handy Textile Excuse-O-Matic

❑ I have my period
❑ It's a free beach
❑ My boyfriend won't let me
❑ I'm from Toronto
❑ I'll burn/I'm burned
❑ I've been coming here my entire life
❑ You just want to see my cock
❑ I have a medical condition/scars
❑ I'll get a hard-on
❑ I'm having laser surgery tomorrow
❑ My pubic hair needs a shave/has a bad shave
❑ I'm not a fag
❑ Other (please specify) _____

from Toronto," "My boyfriend won't let me," "I'm not a fag," and, the ultimate, "You just want to see my cock." None of these, in her opinion, is worth the paper they're not printed on.

There's no denying there's something faintly, well, forbidding about the houses, the White House and its self-described "nude Nazis" in particular. Perhaps the nude Nazis' unspoken lack of enthusiasm for the uninitiated is best exemplified by the fact that, of the White House regulars, the most recent, who has been coming for a mere seventeen years, is known as the new guy.

And still there's more to look at, if you like. The naked, Norse-looking vendor, six and a half feet tall with scrubby blond hair and a little brushy 'stache, trotting his cooler on by. No sign of the cops yet. Very few single women, you've noticed. A fully dressed can collector threading his way between the logs. A truly shocking variety of body shapes and sizes, from the morbidly obese to the frighteningly stringy and everything in between. Every shade of skin from fish belly to ebony. The tanned, the toned — far fewer of these than you'd like — the girls baring only their breasts, the boys shirtless and swathed in the familiar baggy board shorts. Giving nothing away.

Closer to the rocks that form the breakwater, the crowd thins slightly, becomes less of a suffocating press. There are three or four single guys here, dotted around, and one or two male couples, superbly muscled the lot of them, obviously gay. On the whole of the main beach under Trail Six, from the rocks on one side to the breakwater on the other, this is the closest you'll find to a spot where any particular group — in this case, gay men who prefer to stay on the main beach rather than going down the path to the gayside — segregates itself. Otherwise, everyone just mixes, easily or uneasily, from the muscular-looking cyclist accompanied, inexplicably, by his machine (how, and why, did he manage all those steps?) to the European tourist watching it all in blasé fashion — only in puritan North America, he tells himself smugly, would people make such an enormous fuss about what is, after all, only a bit of skin. Everyone comes here, from the pair of tattooed native gals from the Musqueam reserve, another couple, to the pale-skinned students still brandishing (but hardly working on) their homework. The rocks, when you climb up, smell of urine; the far side is an unofficial latrine.

Past the breakwater, the landscape changes abruptly. There's marsh grass on the other side, and muddy, sucking ground under-foot, and the wooded shore slopes away as if ashamed. In the direc-tion you've been walking is the mouth of the Fraser River, where fresh water mixes with salt. Logs are stored here, acres of them, for their final trip upriver to the sawmills. They can't be floated for any length of time in undiluted salt water because of a parasite — the teredo worm, also known as shipworm — that has an insa-tiable appetite for salt-cured wood.

Here also, though you can't see it, is the gay side of the beach. Behind those bushes to your left, around that bend, winds a nar-row, mucky trail leading to a real beach: the Oasis.

The Oasis shows you what this place would look like without human interference. The beach sand there is fine-grained, grey, and pure. It came down from the cliff in a rather spectacular col-lapse about ten years ago. That summer, regulars returned to find the alders buried three feet up their trunks in fine sand.

"Mare-ih-wanna," someone murmurs, passing, as you scramble back down the rocks on the beach side of the breakwater and stand, panting. You turn — too late — and see the vendor heading north without looking back.

There is a small beach at the tip of the breakwater, a hidden one, colonized at weekends by one non-nudist family. Secret Beach, it's called, or Gilligan's Island — you heard about it from a guy who kayaks over here on weekends. At the time you thought, vaguely, that you might like to see it. Close up, however, the rocks look more forbidding than you'd imagined. You decide that today, with the sun beating down, is no time to investigate such matters. A peculiar lassitude has begun to steal over you. You turn your back to the beach and its layer of bodies, run down to the water, and wade in. There's a coldness to it, even in August, that revives you, although you're only in up to your knees. You imagined plunging in headfirst, but there's no drop-off. The sand goes out and out and out, barely sloping away. You're in up to your thighs now, after some energetic wading, but farther out you can see people stand-ing almost completely out of the water. The waves foam and break there against what must be a sandbar hidden by their swell.

You turn back to the shore, where the wavelets swell and break gently against the beach. By letting yourself fall in backwards, you find you can not so much swim as float, the cool ebbing around your ears. You bob a little, looking back at the kaleidoscope: the green of the bluffs, the patchwork tan of bodies, the bright spots of umbrellas and towels. After a few minutes you clamber out and make your way back to your place, where you lie down, full-length and dripping, on your towel. You're starting to feel an unfamiliar sensation, and finally it comes to you as you sip lazily from a tin and, head propped, watch the bodies from beneath the brim of your cap. This is what it's like to have nothing you're required to do. Nothing to do, nowhere to go, no one to bother, no one bothering you.

This, then, you decide, is the genius of the place. Not what you do, but what you don't do: pack a suit, bring your laptop, line up at the concession, run the lifeguard gauntlet at the shoreline. There is a magic here and maybe it's simply that, not so much what is — the sun, the shore, the mountains hazing away on the horizon — as what isn't. Nothing to distract from the world as it should be.

For a while you've been listening with half an ear to the sound of music, enthusiastic and oompah-ish. Finally you raise your head. You see them now, down the beach: an impromptu band strumming guitars, someone toting a drum, everyone in oversize, cartoonish hats. They are collecting change for the Wreck Beach Preservation Society. Its good works, you're aware, are legion: the website, the action updates, and, most importantly, the preservation of the beach. Most everybody involved with the society donates their time, sometimes endless hours of it, attending public input meetings on the university campus, appearing before the board of the Greater Vancouver Regional District, which administers the beach, and doing countless other dreary yet essential tasks. That doesn't mean there aren't costs: printing charges, server space, lawyers. You rummage in your bag and, when a volunteer comes by, drop in a toonie. Let's hope it's the first of many.

Peter Biggs (foreground) and a friend in the Scary Grass behind the breakwater, circa 1979. JAMES LOEWEN PHOTO

TWO

The Other Side

In the popular mind, nudity and sex are indivisible. There is a certain logic to this. Most people get naked when they mean to do the deed, so the sight of another's naked form — especially a stranger's — inspires even the most cynical with a certain, how to put it, hope. In nakedness there is a childish directness, a retreat to a state that is preverbal or at least extra-verbal. Nudity evokes simplicity, pleasure, a concentration on the body. But mostly sex.

For everybody, that is, except the nudist. Brian Watts, a lifelong skin enthusiast and onetime Wreck Beach regular, now frequents the private Van Tan nudist club, the country's oldest, on Vancouver's North Shore. He takes his vacations at far-flung nudist resorts or aboard cruise ships chartered by the Bare is Beautiful crowd. His holiday snaps, freely shown to clients — Watts is an accountant — mostly feature his comely wife Donna as nature made her. Their deck is discreetly fenced and features an outdoor shower. When he is interviewed about Wreck Beach in his home, Watts greets his visitor in a shirt, period. Sitting at a glass-topped table off the comfortable kitchen, he is entirely at ease.

To hear Watts tell it, his nudity has never been an issue. Not when his new mother-in-law dropped in, unannounced, while he was studying naked as a young married student. Not when the neighbourhood kids in his North Vancouver cul-de-sac came over to play with his and Donna's children. Not even when he took those same kids to Wreck Beach. Brian Watts just might be the poster child for nudity as a lifestyle choice, not a precursor to sex.

Nudists have laboured long and hard to dissolve the association between nakedness and sexuality. It is unlikely they will succeed. A posting on the Casual Encounters section of Craigslist, a popular, free, online bulletin board with a Vancouver site, says as much:

> we are a hot and horny couple headed to wreck beach for the day! Would love to spice the day up with an erotic encounter or some company that is willing to play along and see where things might take us! please do not reply if not serious about making or actively participating in . . . well . . . who knows!

Wreck Beach regulars try, with great earnestness, to discourage this sort of thinking.

Judy Williams, introduced in Chapter One, is the blonde, tanned, sixty-something head of the Wreck Beach Preservation Society (WBPS). For a person who spends as much time as possible naked, Williams has a sophisticated understanding of clothes. At government meetings she wears corporate drag: a shapeless navy skirt suit, her pale blonde hair in a severe French twist, black-rimmed spectacles. Photos taken at Wreck Beach over the years show Williams in a variety of other guises. At the beach, her blond plait like a crown above her brow, embroidery in her hands: "Wreck Beach is a Way of Life." Jumping into a wave laughing, nude but for a girlish grass skirt. Nude again on the sand, this time with a kerchief tied over her hair and arms akimbo, looking for all the world like a housewife demonstrating a new washing machine. In her earlobes these days you will notice dangling earrings in the shape of car keys. They *are* car keys, which ensures she'll never lose them.

When it comes to Wreck Beach, Williams is ubiquitous, on speed-dial for city media who need a quote on matters relating to the beach, nude beaches elsewhere, and public nudity in general. Like most nudists, she cannot emphasize enough that nudity is a *family* activity: wholesome, good for you, entirely devoid of sexual content. Like vitamins, but with labia.

Her arguments have not reached everyone. "Once or twice a summer, people go down and try it on," says regular Marilyn Hogan, with evident distaste. Queried further, she elaborates reluctantly: "Open sexuality with whoever they're with."

Judy Williams does not allow such misguided souls to persist in their folly. It's a drizzly winter day, summer barely a memory, when she tells me about a couple she once spotted having sex on the sand in full view of the beach. When they ignored Williams' request that they desist, she began whacking them with her stick. "This is," she remembers telling the male half of the couple, "a family beach." For existing families, that is, not ones you're making.

Williams also recalls coming upon what was obviously a porn shoot in progress. Williams and the other regulars didn't hesitate. Beachers helpfully boxed up the nonplussed film crew's equipment and politely toted it to the stairs. Meanwhile, Williams called 911 and tried to explain to the operator why she should send police. "The filming is getting explicit," she recalls telling her.

The operator, according to Williams, didn't get it. "What do you mean 'explicit'?"

"I mean fucking and sucking!" Williams quotes herself as roaring finally.

Williams can't be everywhere, of course, and even the purest minded of nudists cannot deny the sensual entirely. The landscape inspires blissful repose and, perhaps, thoughts of closeness. Opportunities abound for the resourceful. There are pockets and crannies of bush at the back of the beach, where it is the work

Beach doyenne Judy Williams wears her car keys in her ears and her sentiments on a bumper sticker proclaiming 'Shame on UBC.'
PACIFIC PRESS ARCHIVES

of a moment to retreat from the hot sun and prying eyes. (The small unpleasantness of discovering evidence of others' makeshift latrines will not deter the truly focused.) The enterprising know that a driftwood enclosure rigged with a sheet can be a surprisingly effective cover-up. An amble in the direction of Spanish Banks will reveal plenty of relatively unfrequented spots. The water, to state the obvious, is practically opaque. Those who are sensitive about scaring the children can wait until darkness begins to fall, when most families — most beachgoers, in fact — have gone home.

That's what one ménage of trois did, taking up a discreet position at the back of the beach. Uncharacteristically, regulars, one who was there told me, decided not to stop them but, instead, to relax, perch atop some convenient logs, and enjoy the view.

The ménage was reaching its intricate conclusion as the Can Man was finishing up his rounds. The Can Man was one of the legion of collectors who frequented the beach, so-called because of his habit of singing an annoying little ditty — "Can Man, I'm the Can Man. Give me your cans, man, I'm the Can Man" — as he dragged the beach for tin. The Can Man was almost upon the three enthusiasts before he looked up, saw what he had blundered into, and fled, leaving his precious bag of cans behind.

In spite of popular perception, Wreck Beach is definitely not all about sex. Unless, that is, you're a gay man. The gay side of the beach, beginning from the bush-shrouded trail that threads its way southeast past the breakwater, is its own world. Even the seawater changes here, stirred to a brackish mix by the outflowing Fraser River. The gayside has a unique landscape, specific terminology, particular codes of behaviour, and — for want of a better word — rampant rutting. Long may it prosper.

Entering the gayside after the bright brassiness of the main beach on a summer's day is a shock. The trail is shady and cool and often so narrow that when two men meet, one must stand aside to let the other pass. A rat scurries along branches arcing overhead. The trail twists through underbrush, past fallen trees, over muddy ground and small patches of marsh grass. At unpredictable intervals it widens, offering vistas of the Fraser and the giant booms of logs stored there. Regulars have carved spaces for themselves out of sand and logs or brush; they are equipped with lawn chairs, cans of beer, and brimmed sunhats, like suburban homeowners. These spaces are known as condos.

Rick Fearman is the gayside's unofficial custodian. In 2005 he put down what he calls "mini-bridges" — planks with feet, essentially — which he'd constructed out of scrap wood. These allow people to cross the frequent mudholes on the foreshore trail without getting their feet wet. Fearman has a proprietary pride in the beach's gay section. On the day I visit, he has raked the leaves from the floor of the aspen grove behind Oasis Beach so that the close-grained grey sand is clear but for sandal prints.

The Oasis is the gayside's one sandy bit of waterfront, and it lives up to its name. A row of trees partly screens the view of the beach. One lithe, muscled young man is kissed on the neck by a man who stands behind him. As the sun moves lower in the sky, two naked men move to the shore and stand, arms slung around each other, picture-perfect against the glowing river and silhouetted log booms. There is little swimming here — it's generally clean enough, by measurement, but the mud-coloured water puts most everyone off. Seals pop to the surface offshore, their sleek heads black against the water, and dive again. Regular Brian Baxter says some of his most memorable gayside moments involve wildlife: eagles screaming as they couple in midair; ordinarily territorial giant herons feeding on a single school of fish in a patch of river twenty metres square.

The gayside also has a rich, specific vocabulary. Take, for instance, the chest-high beach grass on the flats. The area is known to habitués variously as Pop Tart Beach or the Scary Grass. Why the names? "Nobody sees you till you stand up," Baxter explains of the first moniker. And the second? "You never know what you're going to find."

Blatant cruising is accepted behaviour on the gayside, and this can lead to some amusing situations. James Loewen, a soft-spoken gay man of fifty-two, has been going to the beach for more than thirty years. He recalls bringing one boyfriend, a transsexual (that is, a man who had formerly been a woman), to the beach. Loewen's date was transitioning; although he looked quite masculine, he still had his original female genitals. When another gay man began cruising the couple, Loewen's boyfriend kept his crotch hidden — so much less work than tedious explanations. This frustrated their would-be admirer, and at last he could stand this apparent coyness no longer. Approaching Loewen's date, he took hold of one knee and gently pulled it aside. In silence, he gazed at the mystery. "You're kind of small, aren't you?" he said finally.

"If people really understood what a paradise Wreck Beach is for gay men, they would shut it down," Loewen remarks. Then he corrects himself. "No. They would want that for themselves."

The area has its inevitable tourists, according to regulars: the occasional gal in high heels; the occasional clued-out, fully clad family; the occasional woman tagging along with her gay friends. Then there are the men, nominally heterosexual and just out for a stroll. Brian Baxter remembers a Greek guy who opened a conversation with "So what goes on down here?" After sex, his nervousness returned. "Now, if you see me on the street, you don't know me," he insisted unnecessarily.

Another sexual episode involved a chiselled beachgoer on the way up Trail Seven. Baxter had cruised him earlier but figured he had no chance. The glances he began getting as they climbed changed his mind. As he moved closer, the other man stopped him: "Okay, but we can't touch." Their entire sexual encounter took place at arm's length. It was, Baxter says with a reminiscent smile, "one of the most erotic experiences."

Public sex is not only allowed on the gayside, it is expected. (Though often it is quasi-public: many gay men will step off the path into semi-screened or fully hidden spots for such activities.) And not just for homosexuals. In fact, one heterosexual couple, famous among gayside regulars, makes the trek from Seattle once or twice a season. The two find their way to the beach-grass area at the far end of the trail — known as Jurassic Park because it's where the older men traditionally gather. There they proceed to have sex in full view of everyone. The gay men who generally form their audience don't mind, mostly because, as one regular explained to me with evident satisfaction, both members of the couple are "stunning."

Let's remember that public sex is illegal. That holds true whether you are on the gay side, the straight side, a teenager in a parked car, or from Seattle. Still, it only became an issue after the Royal Canadian Mounted Police acquired their first openly gay officer. Constable Robert Ploughman, until he was rotated in 2006, was the patrolman in charge of Wreck Beach. With only a summer constable for backup, he routinely confiscated drugs and booze, arrested drunk drivers, hauled miscreants up the 402 steps to the top of Trail Six, called for the hovercraft in cases of heatstroke, and made the long walk down the gayside trail. In 2002, reporter Jeremy Hainsworth wrote in *Xtra West*, the city's gay newspaper, about what happened next:

> In his eight months at Wreck, Ploughman has not seen anyone having sex and knows of no charges being laid. He says he's not going to crawl through dense bush to find people having sex and that finding private places is a matter of common sense.
>
> "If anybody's stupid enough to be doing that graphic sex act right in the middle of the trail, then we'll enforce that law."

Ploughman may not have seen such things, but there were at least two moments during my own tour of gay Wreck Beach when Loewen, my escort, halted. "We'll just go around here," he'd murmur, or "Let's just stop and chat for a few moments." I discreetly averted my eyes from the figures far ahead of us on the path, so I can't really say what they were doing.

Ploughman, who hails from Newfoundland, has a refreshingly elastic view of law and order. His method of patrolling the beach was simple. As Ploughman describes it, he would descend the stairs in full RCMP uniform, seek out beach doyenne Judy Williams, and have a long, highly visible chat with her. Only then would the constable proceed to crisscross the beach, confiscating open cans of beer.

When the time came for that trip down the trail, Ploughman waited until a regular set off from the main beach. He ambled along behind, absentmindedly jingling a large and noisy bunch of keys. Though Ploughman is no nudist — "not since I got stretch marks," he jokes — he's relaxed about the things that make Wreck, in his determinedly value-free phrasing, "unique." And although he asserts that "it wouldn't be safe to go down on my off day," he adds, "I'll miss the people and I'll miss the sunsets" once he is transferred. "I won't miss the heat. I've been up and down the stairs five times in a day with someone fighting in handcuffs the whole way. I feel privileged," he sums up, "having worked down there."

Ploughman is also respectful of the regulars' code of conduct.

"I think it shows ownership by a community when they want to enforce safety standards. They keep an eye out for pedophiles, which we can't do. We can't be everywhere."

If sex is the first thing to inflame the minds of those who've never been to the beach, other illicit activities run a close second. One day, two students from the university are holding what they call a production meeting on the sands, though what exactly they're producing remains unclear to an eavesdropper. "I don't feel like we're getting much work done," says one, sipping her beer thoughtfully. Later she remarks, "It seems like ages since we smoked a joint." The students rectify the error.

Judy Williams would not approve, at least not in principle. "There are three things that's going to kill the beach," Williams says in a coffee shop near the university the same bleak November day she talks about sex on the beach. "Gay sex. Drugs. And drinking. These things happen everywhere, but because we're a nudist beach they're a big deal."

Pot is the mainstay, after beer, of the beach. Some longtime beach regulars eschew it entirely; Korky Day, an engaging perennial hippie who organized the 1970 nude-in that brought the area to prominence, says he has never indulged. However, the *Georgia Straight*'s annual reader's poll consistently ranks Wreck as one of the best places in town to smoke a joint.

The most famous recent vendor of the stuff has to be Watermelon, known legally as Mary Ann Dunstan, arrested in September 2001, amidst great hullabaloo, for selling THC-laced cookies on the beach.

Watermelon is a perfect specimen of feminine pulchritude, all baby-blonde hair, tanned curves, and the kind of wide-eyed, pouffy-lipped good looks that are endlessly mutable: slutty housewife, damsel in peril, Bettie Page-ette, comely Statue of Liberty. She appears regularly on the cover and in the pages of such magazines as the marijuana bible *High Times*. No doubt her pin-up good looks reassure stoner boys that yes, even if they do nothing but sit in their bedrooms smoking pot all day, a goddess of a girl will appear on their doorsteps, proffering more bud.

Still, Watermelon has her detractors. One regular sniffs that she's tried the notorious cookies but they gave her no buzz whatsoever. Another snips that Watermelon doesn't vend on the beach much

*Watermelon was arrested in 2001 for selling ginger cookies with
extra snap. She was busted by the notorious RCMP Constable
'Napoleon' Francoeur. In his right hand is the evidence.* LINCOLN
CLARKES PHOTO

these days. (Understandable, since while charges were pending, staying away from Wreck was one of the conditions of her release.) The charges against Watermelon, by the way, were finally dismissed when analysis found no trace of the particular cannabis residue described in arrest documents in the seized gingersnaps. The lack of a criminal record was nice, but the vendor, who also performs as a comedienne around town, was still stuck with an $18,000 legal bill.

Why are vendors attracted to Wreck? Low start-up costs, no doubt, but more likely the chance, as one beer vendor put it, to make enough money in the season that he doesn't have to work for the rest of the year.

Vendors sell mushrooms as well. These kinder, gentler psychedelics fit in with the let-it-be beach ethos and, as a bonus, can be sourced for free in coastal forests during the fall rainy season by off-the-grid types in gumboots.

Booze has been sold and consumed at the beach for so long that it might be called a tradition, despite intermittent attempts to rein in the trade. Crackdowns started as early as 1983, when a hovercraft normally used for beach rescues assisted in a mass arrest of people selling booze and drugs. "During the 'Great Hovercraft Raid,' as it has become known, a huge crowd materialized quickly when people realized the hovercraft had brought RCMP to the beach," an anonymous writer reported in the next summer's Wreck Beach Committee (later Preservation Society) newsletter. "An angry howl arose that could be heard above the roar of the propeller blades at a quarter mile's distance. Rocks were hurled . . . men leaped aboard." The writer predicted darkly that much ground had been lost in the relationship between beachers and officials.

A certain Constable Francoeur, a Frenchman regulars named Napoleon in reference to his background and maybe to other things as well, was the next to try to staunch the flow. Francoeur decided on an unofficial "three-beer rule." In theory, this meant police would confiscate booze from vendors but not from those who had simply brought a few cans for personal consumption. The system was only partially successful. Some beachgoers, faced with a coolerful of evidence, claimed an ever-expanding group of friends, each entitled to his ration of three.

The skirmishes continue to this day. In the summer of 2006,

new officers were patrolling the beach. An altercation with an obnoxious drunk ended with one officer grinding the beachgoer's face into the sand. A crowd gathered to advise the police on what onlookers judged to be their use of excessive force. The next weekend an RCMP helicopter buzzed the beach. Incensed WBPS members who called the detachment could find nobody who had authorized the flyby.

There have been plenty of creative attempts to avoid those pesky police patrols and attendant confiscation of alcohol. Regular James Loewen, the vice-chair of the WBPS, noticed some people standing up to their shoulders in the sand on the main beach one day and went to investigate. Under a log he discovered a tiki bar complete with counter, giant head with light-up eyes, and sound system. If someone had rigged up a blender, they could have been in business.

The beach has had periodic influxes of harder drugs, probably because dealers realized there was relatively little law enforcement on the sands below the university. The area at the bottom of Trail Six is still known as the Pharmacy. At one time, beachgoers had to run a gauntlet of dealers as they emerged onto the sand and made for the logs. Donna Watts, a former regular, remembers that the mood of the place began to change around five o'clock. People were falling-down drunk, and the drumming had started. Watts and her husband, who came with their small children, disliked the transformation. Eventually they stopped going entirely.

Most regulars agreed with Watts. They were dismayed by the increasing presence of hard drugs, mostly cocaine. Officers from the UBC RCMP detachment argued that part of the reason drugs had become a problem was the lack of easy police access to the beach. Their solution: bulldoze a path for patrol cars. "Drug sales and buying spur road threat!" was a headline in the 1991 *Wreck Beach News*, the free newsletter (later fitted up with the slogan "All the Nudes that's Fit to Print") distributed to beachgoers once or twice a summer by the WBPS. (The road idea has been raised every few years but never gets past the starting gate. It's discussed in more detail in Chapter Four.)

In the early 1990s, when the problem was at its height, Korky Day organized a beach debate on the subject of drugs. Ignoring beach etiquette, he didn't ask Judy Williams first. "Maybe it was one of those times when she wasn't speaking to me much for some other reason," Day says today. Williams boycotted the debate, which according to Day she called "the most hare-brained scheme you've come up with yet." Fifteen people showed up, and not all at once, either. "At the moment," says Day of Williams, warily, "we're on good terms." And the drug dealers, for their part, are far less visible than they once were.

There have been other clashes between competing groups of users. According to writer Dennis Bolen, another longtime beach-goer, there were "one or two years in the mid-90s when it seemed to be that the Surrey tattooed-pit-bull set discovered Wreck Beach. These guys liked it," Bolen hypothesizes, "because they could bring their German horror dogs down to the beach and let them run free."

Regulars continue to complain about usurpers of one kind or another. In the summer 2000 issue of the *Wreck Beach News*, letter-writer Jim Steiger said that skimboarders had "invaded the beach, and . . . are starting to create hazardous conditions . . . The younger folk seem more interested in working out aggression and showing off than they do in 'melding in' to our community."

Wreck Beach has inspired not only dog lovers, not only people lovers, not only pot lovers, but also lovers of the dark. The tradition is a longstanding one. Musqueam elder Larry Grant recalls visiting the beach in 1948 and 1949 with other native teenagers for bonfires. Twenty years later, in a February 27, 1969, article in the Vancouver *Province*, Dr. William Gibson, the head of the department of medicine and science history at UBC, remarked that, in the summer, the beaches below the university were "a hangout for hippies and the litter of gin bottles left after Saturday nights has to be seen." In the same article, the *Province* characterized the beach as a "student lovers' retreat and beach party mecca." An unsigned article in the summer 1982 issue of the WBPS newsletter complained of "grim reminders of loud and rough night groups . . . Few logs have escaped fire scars. Too often fires smoulder for days. Night people seem neither to care nor to understand that these fires with shattered glass cannot be covered up."

The night people are a headache to pretty much everyone but themselves. Watermelon worries about the messes they leave, but she is also concerned that a UBC student, drunk or high, will wan-

der into the water and drown. She sees their carelessness as another threat to the beach, an excuse for authorities to shut it down.

Greater Vancouver Regional District rules require that visitors leave the beach by sunset, but the nightly gathering is often reluctant to disperse. "It gets ugly after that," says Constable Ploughman when asked about clearing the beach. "It's the most dangerous thing we do out there." One time Ploughman and a patrol partner were hauling a detainee up the Trail Six steps to Marine Drive when they looked ahead. A crowd with lighted torches was descending towards them. The two officers ordered the crowd back. At the top of the steps, Ploughman says, the would-be partiers saw that "there were 600 of them and two of us. Beer bottles started flying." Ploughman doesn't reveal how that situation turned out, but he says that Wreck Beach regulars have saved him "more than once."

Victimless crime may be the norm, but not everyone escapes scot-free. In 1974, Wreck made the news when a twenty-seven-year-old told would-be muggers he was out of cash. He was beaten. Occasionally a beer vendor who tries to undercut the competition is roughed up by his fellows. In the main, however, "a lot of the problems have not been from regular beachers," says longtime

This spar was a feature of the beach under Trail Four in the 1970s. The North Shore mountains can be seen behind. DON SLADE PHOTO

regular Marilyn Hogan. "Tourists, teenagers, people who get the
idea that 'anything goes' at the beach. It gets documented, and it
skews public perception of what it's really like down there."

Wreck Beach has rarely been the site of more serious crime.
The most serious of all — murder — has only occurred twice. In
1990, Kevin Ladouceur, a drifter and small-time marijuana dealer
who went by the dubious nickname "Scummy," died of a ruptured
spleen after a beating. Four men were arrested for his slaying.
Afterwards, Judy Williams made the uncharacteristic statement
that "more policing was needed" on the beach. Marina, a WBPS
member who would give only her first name, told a *Globe and
Mail* reporter, "The people that were responsible for the death
are not really a part of the beach." Then she added the clincher:
"They're not nudists."

In 1993, Christina Joy Thompson, a vendor known as Topless
Tina, was killed as she came up the steps after a day at the beach.
Thompson's killer later confessed to the murder. The crime
shocked beachers and inspired a play titled *Wreck Beach* that was
loosely based on the killing. It garnered lukewarm reviews. At least
one reviewer pointed out that producers had failed to consult with
the family of the victim. On the second night of the play's run in
2000, Korky Day bought a ticket, found a seat, and removed his
clothes. The director came out from the backstage area to remon-
strate with him. Day suggested the matter be put to a vote; if the
audience decreed, he would rerobe. The other playgoers saw his
point. The vote went in his favour and Day remained nude.

Other deaths at the beach have been accidental. In June 1974 a
young man drowned after he waded out to the breakwater and was
trapped by an incoming tide. One year later a diver broke his neck
and was paralyzed. In 1978 another bather drowned, despite the
efforts of other swimmers to save him. The park board, then the
nominal overseer of the beach, subsequently voted down a proposal
to fund lifeguards for the area. Commissioner Evelyn Atkinson
unwisely explained the board's thinking. "We were also concerned
about what a lifeguard would hold on to if a drowning person did
not have a bathing suit on." (In another article, Atkinson described
herself as "so conservative, I sleep on my right side.")

That summer, a lifeguard named Craig Jacks took it upon himself to begin patrolling Wreck Beach as a volunteer. He wore a

T-shirt, yellow sunhat, and nothing else. Jacks's effort did not last long, but possibly because of the main beach's shift from Trail Four to Trail Six, where the water is comparatively calm, drownings are no longer an issue. Bodies are still occasionally dumped on the beach, however. A couple out for a stroll discovered one in October 2006. The clean-cut, middle-aged man had been killed elsewhere, and his body, in a sleeping bag, washed ashore.

The occasional medical emergency — a heart attack, a broken arm, sunstroke, or the supremely out-of-shape person who has made it down the trail but cannot get up again — falls to the Coast Guard hovercraft, which is on hand to evacuate victims. If the mishap turns out to be the beachgoer's own fault, as was the case for the obese guy who misjudged his ability to re-climb the stairs, the hapless evacuee can be charged the cost of his rescue: up to $1,000.

As you'd expect, it's the human factor that is most significant in the beach experience, at least today. But nature once did, and may again, play a far larger role.

THREE

The Making of the Beach

Wreck Beach got its name in 1928, according to a letter lodged in Vancouver's city archives. Three "log barges and a floating grain elevator — the 'Biscayne', 'Bingamon', 'Black Wolf', and the 'Blatchford' — operated by the Pacific Tug and Barge Company, were towed around to the North Arm of the Fraser River to act as a breakwater for a large log storage ground." They were sunk off what is now the main beach below Trail Six.

There have been, and continue to be, a number of other names for the area. Korky Day occasionally calls the area Ulksen Beach. Ulksen means "point of land" in Halkomelem, the traditional language of the Musqueam people, and the nomenclature is intended as a nod to the Musqueam, for whom the beach is unceded territory. Tower Beach refers to the site of two Second World War-era searchlight towers that were built when the city feared the possibility of an attack by Japanese submarines. Acadia Beach is the section closest to Spanish Banks. The area has also been called University Beach, presumably for its proximity to campus, and Point Grey Beach, in reference to the entire peninsula. Judy Williams has mentioned that when she first visited the beach in 1971, the specific area she went to was called Coward's Cove. And then there are the nicknames regulars have bestowed on various spots over the years, from the Condos — sheltered nooks around the northern corner from the main beach and partway up the slope, which beachgoers use for winter sunning — to the Oasis, the gayside's largest stretch of sandy waterfront.

According to a university history posted online, the Musqueam,

Before there were formal trails, people slid, ran or tumbled down — and later, clambered back up — the slopes of the now-bare cliffs to get to the beach. DON SLADE PHOTO

Playing in the surf was more fun — and more dangerous — in the 1970s. Wave action eventually washed away most of the sand under Trail Four.
DON SLADE
PHOTO

who still live in the area, originally harvested shellfish and crabs on the beaches of the peninsula, and also used them for launching canoes. In the online history, Emma Spenner Norman, a geography student at UBC, identifies the area below Trail Four as a traditional place of defence, a vantage point from which to watch for approaching Haida or Squamish war canoes. Two forts were constructed here. One, near the present site of the Museum of Anthropology, was where a Musqueam warrior named Kiplen xw lived with one of his several families in the years before European contact. The other, smaller fort was on the beach below. The band never ceded title to the peninsula and still claims the entire Endowment Lands, including Pacific Spirit Park, as Musqueam territory.

In 1923, after demonstrations by students fed up with makeshift quarters, the University of British Columbia began building a new, permanent campus in Point Grey. The granite used to construct the science building and the library was quarried on Nelson Island, north of Vancouver off the Sunshine Coast, and barged to the waterfront. It was then hauled from the bottom of the cliffs to the campus above via an aerial tramway. The clearcut path up is visible in archival photos. A 1927 aerial shot (see p. 61) shows a still largely undeveloped campus with wide patches of bare earth visible on the otherwise treed cliffs. By 1944, another aerial photo, reproduced on p. 56, shows these patches partially grown in.

There are differing views as to when the beach became a haven for nudists. Regulars claim that nude sunbathing was a tradition there as far back as the 1920s, but evidence for this is scanty. One of the only substantiated accounts comes from then-teenage friends Allan Walsh and Albert Robson, who visited the beach in the summers of 1930 and 1931. According to Walsh's account, lodged now in the City of Vancouver's archives, the two did their exploring nude, but "if any people appeared in the distance, we donned our clothes before they got near us." In a special sixtieth-anniversary issue of the *Ubyssey*, the UBC student paper, Malcolm McGregor, a student and staffer at the paper from 1929 to 1931, made jocular mention of the secret, all-male "Society of Thoth," which existed during his time there. He claims to have been among the "first habitués of what is now Wreck Beach," but he does not mention nudity.

There may have been other nude beaches in Vancouver at that time. A 1957 novel by Ronald Hambleton, *Every Man Is an Island*, refers to Douk Beach in a cove by Stanley Park's Siwash Rock. According to the novel, the beach was a haven for unemployed labourers in the 1920s, and its name alludes to the Doukhobors, who removed their clothes during political protests. (Other Greater Vancouver nude beaches continue to surface. Brunswick Bay, on Lion's Bay north of West Vancouver, has been the subject of zealous attempts by locals to ban non-resident parking and otherwise discourage visiting nudists. There's also Crescent Rock Naturist Beach, south of Crescent Beach in White Rock, where, in 2006, Surrey mayor Diane Watts officially asked nude sunbathers to cover up. Bridgeview Reach, a tiny nudist haven on the Fraser River, was inadvertently exposed when a local salvage company cleared brush from the river bank that same year.)

In the mid-1940s, the cliff top acquired its first year-round residents when soldiers moved into Fort Point Grey, above what is now Tower Beach. The fort featured concrete gun turrets, a tunnel, a power station, watchtowers equipped with searchlights, wood-frame officers' and nurses' quarters, and garages. The guns were removed in 1948, and two years later the structures were officially renamed Fort Camp. They became a residence for UBC students, "the site of water fights, bed races and some lively protests over poor student housing conditions," according to Michelle Cook, writing in the September 2001 issue of *UBC Reports*. Cook also mentioned the residence's "dodgy heating" and "drafty walls." The Fort Camp barracks were levelled in 1974.

Larry Grant, a Musqueam elder, was a teenager in the late 1940s when he and his pals went to the beach. They built bonfires and held singalongs. The hulks sunk in 1928 were still visible, but Grant does not remember seeing any naked people in the vicinity. Historically speaking, the question of nudity would have been irrelevant to the Musqueam anyhow. "Our people never really gave it a thought about being covered up or not [until contact with Europeans]," Grant explains.

Van Tan nudist club member Brian Watts, now sixty-seven, grew up in Point Grey. As a child he climbed the sand cliffs above Wreck Beach and skinny-dipped in the sea with other kids from the neighbourhood. He remembers the beach in the late 1940s and early 1950s as being fairly deserted, with the occasional glimpse of a naked person.

The next major human modification of beach geography took place in the mid-1950s when a breakwater was constructed to provide shelter for log booms. The breakwater, which is still a major feature of the beach, is a boulder barrier that separates today's main beach from the marshy Fraser estuary that is Wreck's unofficial gayside. Originally, the breakwater served another purpose. The north arm of the Fraser River ends in a delta; that is, fresh water disperses at the river's mouth to mix with salt water. The breakwater, extending parallel to the river's mouth, prevented this water from spreading over a wider area. As a result, the outgoing channel was worn deeper by the swifter, stronger flow of water. A 1977 dredging operation took up more of the river bottom. The dredged sand, dumped on the north side of the breakwater, became the foundation of present-day Wreck Beach.

Photographer Don Slade, who has taken thousands of photos of Wreck Beach from the 1970s to the present, recalls that nudity was extremely rare in the beach's early days. In 1963, for instance, he took a girlfriend to the beach. She shed her top but was so worried about being caught that she made him post a lookout for her. Slade says he had "gone down [to the beach] lots of times before [1970] and never seen any nude people," so he isn't surprised that two articles about the beach published in 1965 don't mention nudity. The stories appeared in *UBC Reports*, the administration's mouthpiece, and argued for and against plans to build a road on the beach and put backfill in front of the cliffs. (These plans, and the resulting protest, are discussed in more detail in Chapter Four.)

Beachgoers realized one of the rationales for building an access road to the beach was litter removal, so in 1969 a group calling itself Public Concerns began to sponsor regular beach cleanups. These continue, under Preservation Society auspices, to this day.

By 1970, the beach had finally become an acknowledged hot spot for nude sunbathing and the hippie lifestyle. The publicity that established it in this position began with an article in the *Georgia Straight*, a counterculture weekly. "It is common for people to go through a few head changes when they start going nude. Usually by late afternoon at Wreck Beach the feeling is pretty relaxed," "Mr. Natural," AKA Korky Day, told a reporter for an August issue. Day's inside knowledge was remarkable given that he had not yet been to the beach. In the same article, Day mentioned a petition signed by more than 500 people that called for the legalization of beach nudity.

Not everyone was of the same opinion. "We've been getting

A panorama from the tower at the north end of Tower Beach shows the sweep of sand circa 1970. DON SLADE PHOTO

The view of Wreck Beach, looking north from the south tower, early 1970s. The north tower is barely visible behind trees at the right edge of the picture. DON SLADE PHOTO

complaints all year from residents of the area that they can't use the beach because the nudists have taken over," explained an RCMP spokesman in an August 13 *Vancouver Sun* article.

Day, an American import who sold the *Georgia Straight* on street corners to support himself, had already read in that paper about the concept of "free" beaches. He asked around: did Vancouver have one? Nobody knew of any, so Day decided to create one. He announced a nude-in, to be held at Stanley Park's Third Beach on the third weekend of August.

On August 12, the RCMP raided Wreck Beach, arresting thirteen naked sunbathers seemingly at random. The thirteen were tried at University Hill court, on the UBC campus above the beach. Judge M.E. Ferguson levied one fifty-dollar fine and one short jail term. "Nudity in the theatre, night clubs, and in magazines is different because the public has a choice of seeing them or not seeing them," opined the judge. (This led writers at the *Ubyssey,* to point out that anyone who wanted to see naked people at Wreck Beach had to scramble down the side of a cliff to do so.)

Meanwhile, people were calling the *Georgia Straight* to ask why the nude-in wasn't being held at Wreck Beach. News of the arrests and of the nude-in's switch in venue from Third to Wreck ran in the next two editions of the weekly paper. "It is the traditional nude beach and the general public has less chance to be offended at a secluded place," Day told the *Straight* to explain the switch.

Korky Day visited Wreck Beach for the first time on the day of the nude-in. "I slept in, got there late," he shrugs. "I was twenty-two. What do you expect?" Day counted a grand total of 2,000 protesters over the course of the day. The *Vancouver Sun* put the number at 209. Outnumbering the protesters by a factor of ten, again according to the *Sun*, were onlookers in boats who had come to watch. The protesters made their feelings about these latter known: they threw rocks at them. The protest was otherwise peaceful.

In the wake of the nude-in, the arrested nudists, aside from one beachgoer who opted to plead guilty, decided to appeal. They secured for their defence a young lawyer who already had a reputation as a left-leaning progressive, even though he had been called to the bar barely six months before. Today Don Rosenbloom is semi-retired, with a full head of steely hair and burnished-looking skin. He speaks in the full sentences and stentorian voice-of-God tones that one imagines go down especially well in the courtroom. "[Nudity] had been tolerated for so long that nobody imagined there would be a sudden turn of events leading to prosecution," he explains. "There was absolutely no controversy leading up to those prosecutions. One would have thought there'd be some notice."

Rosenbloom decided to take for his test case a young married woman named Sheila Beaupré. The RCMP had entered a picture of Beaupré lying on her front as evidence. "She had a beautiful body," Rosenbloom recalls, adding, "Obviously I was going to take a female over a male."

Rosenbloom sent volunteers from the Free Beach Defence Fund to girlie shows and to buy what were genteelly called "men's magazines" from corner stores. He planned to put the volunteers on the stand, eliciting the information that views of the naked human body were freely available if you knew where to look. If that didn't wash, he would argue that the naked body was not in itself indecent. But the case was eventually won on a legal point. The police had charged beachgoers with indecency. The correct charge, Rosenbloom contended, was being nude in a public place.

The lawyer figured he knew why the RCMP hadn't used the latter. In order to charge someone with being nude in a public place, the police required the consent of the Attorney General. This wasn't required for a charge of indecency. Rosenbloom guessed that the AG's consent wasn't forthcoming. In any event, the judge agreed with him about the inaccuracy of the charges and dismissed them and the beachgoers.

The Defence Fund published an accounting in the *Georgia Straight* the next March. Don Rosenbloom had received a princely $57.20 in fees. That summer, an RCMP spokesman told the *Vancouver Sun* that even though the university detachment had received six complaints about nudity on the beach that year, the provincial Attorney General would not allow them to lay charges under section 159 of the Criminal Code, being nude in a public place. Rosenbloom's surmise had been correct.

"I really do believe that lawsuit freed the beach," Rosenbloom says today. Not for him, though. "I was a regular," says the lawyer, who first visited the beach in 1965, "and I stopped going down right after I won that case because it became Coney Island. It was a double-edged sword for me." He hasn't been back since.

"Every time it got in the papers," explains another former regular, Brian Watts, "more people went down there."

As the beach grew in popularity, the sands at the bottom of Trail Four, once expansive enough to make this prime beachfront, were slowly being washed northwards, around the point. People were still using the area in the mid-1970s — Don Slade's photos from the time show entire families frolicking in the swells — but their margin of sand was shrinking, and the action was shifting to the area below Trail Six.

People had also begun to camp along the beach, building makeshift driftwood shelters. A newspaper photo from the era shows one such shelter, an ID-holding hand extended from it to a police officer doing a sweep of the area. But by 1974 the RCMP was downplaying the issues raised by permanent beachers. Despite what a *Province* reporter estimated as thirty-five beach campsites, nobody wanted to do anything about the squatters. As park board chairman Art Cowie said, "Who's going to tell [the RCMP] to enforce [the beach camping prohibition]? Not me." An unnamed RCMP spokesman said there were few complaints about drugs or drinking. "I'd say the biggest complaint we get is thefts," he said, adding, "What that beach really needs is less publicity and then maybe less people would hear about it."

It was something of an unofficial rite of passage for UBC students to spend the night. Paul Young, now the director of planning and design at the UBC Properties Trust, was a UBC student himself in the early 1970s. He remembers attempting to camp out on Wreck with two friends one night. They woke at 3 AM. The tent they'd secured to an overhanging branch was bowed down with rain, and the incoming tide was flooding their sleeping area.

In 1977, the geography of the beach changed abruptly. A quar-

Over the years people have camped on Wreck. Peter (last name unknown) was a denizen in the late 70s. Behind him is a gayside condo — a small encampment. JAMES LOEWEN PHOTO

ter of a million cubic yards of sand — material recovered when
the north arm of the Fraser River was dredged, and known unro-
mantically as "dredgate" — was dumped in the crook of the L
of sand and rocks below Trail Six. Sheltered by the breakwater,
it remained. Korky Day recalls that, when summer came, other
beachgoers complained that the newly dumped sand smelled bad.
Day didn't notice the smell; he had a more immediate problem:
concretions. These were fist-size concrete tailings that had been
left in the unsifted dredgate. They were spun into fantastic shapes
by water action, embedded with rocks, and, more to the point,
exquisitely painful to the unshod foot. Day once wasted an hour
concocting a term to describe them in a Wreck Beach newsletter.
The eventual winning adjective? "Lumpy."

That was also the year city councillor Bernice Gerard decided to
take on the beach. Gerard, a Pentecostal preacher, was one more
in an unbroken line of colourful BC politicians. Her announce-
ment that she would walk the beach, along with followers from
her congregation, in a Sunday protest aroused a silly-season storm
of press. At least two media personalities — a radio talk-show
host and a Vancouver Sun columnist — promised to meet Gerard
there in the buff. (Neither showed.) In a letter to the Sun, Gerard
revealed her reason for the protest. According to her, "the nudist
takeover alienates this natural paradise from the average citizen."

The march went ahead as scheduled on July 10, with fully
clad churchgoers trudging along the sand as beachers watched,
bemused. "I just don't like the idea of naked people on the beach,"
explained one of Gerard's protesters after admitting to a reporter
that he'd never previously been there and wouldn't come again.
Afterwards, Gerard claimed that the most offensive mail she
received at the time came from "militant homosexuals who evi-
dently had staked out their territory on the beach."

Korky Day recruited his own protesters, a young man and
woman, on the bus on the way to the beach that day. They wore
matching paper fig leaves over their genitals, hand-printed with
the words "Gerard's Shame." That night, Day went to a friend's
house to watch himself on the television news. As the segment
came on, he realized that the cameras — which he'd assumed
would film him from the waist up — were in fact recording him
in his entirety.

Alderwoman and evangelical preacher Bernice Gerard led a march against nudity in 1977. Korky Day fixed up two fellow beachgoers with these homemade signs as a counter-protest. WAYNE LEIDEN-FROST PHOTO / PACIFIC PRESS ARCHIVES

Other politicians agreed with Gerard, even if they were not planning a protest march to say so. The *Province* of March 21, 1978,
quoted Vancouver park board commissioner Russ Fraser scolding
presenters from the Wreck Beach advisory committee. "You want
a private beach at public expense while you are breaking the law
with your nudity," Fraser said. "You are showing a bit of cheek and
you can take that from both points of view."

In 1989, Bill Vander Zalm, the province's colourful and out-
spoken premier, granted the University Endowment Lands to
the public as Pacific Spirit Regional Park. Vander Zalm had once
pointed out that Jesus "never had a UBC education," so this lavish
gesture should not have been a surprise. There was only one small
problem from UBC's point of view. The Endowment Lands, which
included Wreck Beach, were so called because the provincial government had ceded them to the university when it was established
in 1907. The plan was that UBC would sell land to finance its
development. While some lands, including undeveloped portions
of campus, remained in the university's hands, a swathe of prime
acreage had been taken from it in one fell swoop.

Since 1989, the Greater Vancouver Regional District has been
in charge of the park and Wreck Beach, and it has done little to
change the landscape. There are better trails, with boxed-in steps
and occasional unobtrusive railings. Signage has been standard-
ized and, although unassuming, clearly indicates such crucial
matters as where clothing-optional boundaries begin and end.
Permanent vendors have licences. But that's about it. "We understand the character of the beach, and we understand its unique-
ness," says Mitch Sokalski, the west area manager of the GVRD.
Sokalski himself studied at UBC and remembers going with his
friends to investigate the "nudie" beach for the first time as a student. He even ran down the cliffs on occasion, no doubt hastening
their deterioration (see Chapter Four).

Post-park, anything the GVRD has done has been done carefully
and after extensive consultation with current beach users. Shortly
after it assumed authority over the park, for example, the GVRD
board directed staff to explore the possibility of creating clothed
and unclothed zones on Wreck Beach. To gauge demand for
the scheme, Preservation Society members did a count of naked
and clad beachgoers. The numbers came back practically even:

48 percent unclothed, 52 percent clothed. The zones idea died a quiet death. Sokalski is ever mindful of his mandate. "We're a public agency," he explains. "There was no appetite by the public to change what the typical beach operation was."

The users least satisfied with the beach's current official status are, surprisingly, those who would never think of wearing clothes to the beach. "The absolute worst thing that ever happened was when it became officially recognized as a clothing-optional beach," declares Precious Hutchinson, the regular who compiled the list of excuses people give for not taking it all off. Brian Watts, the one-time Wreck regular who hasn't made the trek down the stairs for a decade, thinks publicity and its official status have killed the beach. "I think when it became, quote, legal, and clothed people started coming down, it [Wreck] got worse," he tells me. "They think it's their beach." The GVRD takeover of Wreck Beach, he says, was the "kiss of death. True nudists enjoy the sun, enjoy the beach. The people now? Sometimes I wonder."

These days, nudity in Vancouver barely raises an eyebrow. Conrad Schmidt, the local organizer of the annual World Naked Bike Ride, is a soft-spoken South African with a penchant for using public performance to dramatize issues of climate change and overconsumption. As Schmidt reported to *Nude and Natural*, the Naturist Society's house organ, after the 2005 ride: "At this stage the police just ignore us. One police car pulled up and said, 'You guys should be wearing helmets.' He didn't even comment on the fact that the people were naked." Other officials took the same tack. As the ride wound its way along the bike path above English Bay in downtown Vancouver, the ranks of cyclists parted to make way for a park board lifeguard handing out sachets of SPF 30, gratis. "Enjoy the ride. Protect your skin," he said, cheerfully.

Mitch Sokalski echoes this impression. He points out that in the last fifteen years there have been fewer than a dozen complaints, in total, about "alternative lifestyles" in Pacific Spirit Regional Park. In fact, complaints about nudity at Wreck these days are more likely to arise from thwarted expectations. First-timers are often volubly disappointed. Instead of the bevy of nude beauties they expected to see, they complain, Wreck Beach is chockablock with wrinkly hippies. Judy Williams would no doubt be pleased to hear it.

The Point Grey peninsula in 1944. UBC ARCHIVES 1543

FOUR

The Top of the Hill

In 1965, the University of British Columbia was already eyeing possibilities for development at Wreck Beach. The administration's proposal that year included a road to the beach, plus backfill in front of the cliffs as an erosion-control measure. A crowd of students estimated at a hundred demonstrated against the plan.

This small skirmish, minor in itself, nonetheless set the pattern for the next four decades. The elements of every future battle were already in place. Administrators, public officials, and big institutions would attempt to have their way with Wreck Beach; small, ad-hoc groups of citizens, students, nature lovers, and nudists would rise up to protect what they saw as the essential character of the beach.

That Wreck Beach has remained, despite the vendors and the driftwood enclosures, one of the least developed beaches in the Lower Mainland is no accident. Other beaches have plumbed washrooms, concession stands filling the air with the smell of hot fat, giant garbage bins next to the sands, bicycle paths, parking lots, and lifeguards perched on tall red chairs. English Bay is regularly bulldozed by little tractors that push the driftwood against which people like to sit into neat, obedient rows. People come to Jericho or Spanish Banks to have enormous barbecues with their families. The police run all-terrain vehicles along the paved walkways at Kits Beach. A host of posted signs above Third Beach describe the rules: No dogs, fires, or inflatable water toys; Children within arms' reach; Alcohol and nudity forbidden. They let you go in the water, but only just.

Wreck Beach has no such infrastructure, unless you count a rank of outhouses in a hidden clearing partway up the Trail Six stairs or the driftwood-outlined concessions at the back of the beach. Its supporters are glad of it. The people who form today's Wreck Beach Preservation Society (WBPS) remember the heady early days and in many ways have never lost their ideals. James Loewen, the society's current vice-chair, can still recall his first-ever act of beach activism. One day shortly after he had begun going to the beach in the early 1970s, he noticed a new, official sign at the top of Trail Seven: Wreck Beach Trail. Loewen drove back that night, stood on his car, and covered the sign with black paint.

Signage has been an issue, trails have been an issue, but the biggest issue — nominally — has been cliff erosion. It turns out that erosion, as a topic, is convenient. It's a catch-all category, able to encompass such apparently unrelated matters as the rowing course, marina, and access road the university wanted to build on the beach below campus in 1965.

The tramway used to haul stones from the waterfront to build the university left a scar on the hillside. UBC ARCHIVES 1818

The bluffs above Wreck Beach are made out of sand. They are called feeder cliffs because the material from the cliffs forms the beaches below. These cliffs erode in one of two ways: from above and from below. In the first instance, rain falls on the cliff tops. Point Grey is an aquifer, which means that the peninsula is composed of multiple layers of sand, rock, and soil. Unless something is in place to stop it, like a building or a paved surface, rainfall and runoff drain through these layers. They trickle or gush out the cliffsides and eventually reach the sea. In the second process, waves break against the bottom of the cliff, eating away what's known as its "toe." These processes are both natural; if the entire peninsula was cleared of humans and their edifices tomorrow, they would continue. "The cliffs [above Wreck Beach] were always eroding, they were always sliding, they were always slumping," says Les Lavkulich, a professor emeritus in UBC's Institute for Resources, Environment and Sustainability.

The peninsula is also inherently unstable. This does not mean a chunk of the cliff is likely to shear off into the sea any time soon, but it does mean that when there is what geologists refer to as an unusual rainfall event — a torrential storm to you and me — a giant fissure can crack open across the campus, as happened in 1935 after days of heavy rain. "Graham's Gully," named for the owner of the house it passed by, carved a path from the intersection of Chancellor and Marine Drive to Tower Beach. Brush has grown over the gulch, but it exists to this day.

Cliff erosion can be hastened or slowed, as you'd expect, by human intervention. When surfaces on campus are paved, for example, rain can no longer seep slowly into the soil. Instead, it is channelled into storm sewers as runoff. These sewers bypass the natural trickle-down effect and increase runoff's erosive power. Meanwhile, if the aquifer's delicate balance shifts too far one way or the other, it behaves the same way as a giant sandcastle. Too dry, it crumbles: too wet, it slumps. There have been some notable cliffside slumps recently, like the one above the Oasis that raised the level of the beach, another in 1997 below Cecil Green Park House near Trail Four, and three in 2004 and 2005 that the WBPS claims are linked to building activity on the campus above.

The cliffs have also been subject to individual indignities. Students once marked their love affairs or graduation years by carving initials and dates into the soil; these remained for years until they crumbled away or were obscured by vegetation. Vancouver writer Stan Persky noted in a 1976 short story that, "in self-sculpted layers of the crumbling cliff, kids and maybe lovers had scrambled along precarious ledges to inscribe their names." By the mid-1960s, portions of the cliffs were entirely bare of vegetation, gently rounded, and striated. Students liked to run, bound, or even roll down them on their way to the beach. Before the trails were upgraded by the Greater Vancouver Regional District after 1989, and to a lesser extent even today, beachgoers also created unofficial or goat trails. These were made for convenience — like the one between Trails Six and Seven, which was apparently constructed, at great effort, by two dedicated beachgoers — or for less innocent purposes. They are useful, for instance, if you are hauling large coolers of beer down to the beach to sell and you wish to avoid the attentions of RCMP officers inconveniently posted at the top of Trail Six, checking everyone's rucksacks.

The area of most concern to university officials, erosion-wise, is the spot between the two searchlight towers on Tower Beach. The university has a showpiece mansion, Cecil Green Park House, on the bluffs above that part of the beach. Built in 1912, the home was known as "Kanakla," "Langara," and finally "Yorkeen" before it was donated to the university by alumnus Cecil Green in 1967. According to current house manager Anne Merling, the property has lost approximately two-thirds of its grounds to erosion since it was built, and the shrinking of the cliff-top lawns is visible to longtime staffers. Graham's Gully, the gulch that opened in 1935, is next to nearby Green College, a reminder of the damage a catastrophic cliff-top failure could cause.

The Vancouver park board, which was in charge of the beach prior to the GVRD takeover, was, like UBC, pro-development. In 1967 the board unveiled its plans for a beach road, much like the one that still skirts Spanish Banks. There was immediate public debate. Maria Furstenwald, an assistant professor of German at UBC and a member of the anti-development group Public Concerns, contributed an article to the *Ubyssey* in which she wrote that she shed "bitter tears" at the sight of preliminary dumping of fill on what she called Vancouver's last "virgin" beach. Furstenwald also complained that it was difficult for the group to obtain

information about the park board's plans. "Secrecy, in-camera decisions, contradictions, inconsistencies, evasive and misleading answers to the public, partisan attitude to civic groups — all this indicates our elected representatives are not doing their job very well." She urged students to "become involved in the political process" to save the beach from development.

Students formed a human chain to stop bulldozing in February 1967, and an anti-road petition signed by nearly 5,000 residents was delivered to the premier. That same year the *Vancouver Sun* pegged the rate of cliff erosion at three inches annually. The figure might have come from a 1962 report by local engineering firm Swan Wooster. (A report in 1976 put the recession rate higher, at six to eighteen inches a year.)

Also in 1967, an architect named Vladimir Plavsic drew up plans for student housing, a group of pueblo-style dwellings on the cliffside above the beach. His proposal included multiple funiculars and a pedestrian tunnel under Marine Drive. The *Ubyssey* reported that Plavsic had not consulted students nor studied campus housing needs before publicizing his ideas. The proposal went nowhere.

The plans for a beach road continued to be an issue into 1969 and beyond. Student Niels von Meyenfeldt struck a conciliatory tone in an opinion piece published in the February 27 issue of

Point Grey peninsual in 1927. Extensive scarring on the bluffs left by construction had largely healed over by 1944 — see the photo on p. 56. UBC ARCHIVES 885-2

the university administration's paper, *UBC Reports*. "Most people agree that the rowing course and marina are needed, that the erosion of the cliffs must indeed be checked, and that University Beach requires improvements to make it attractive and accessible to the public at large." But von Meyenfeldt criticized the plan for a road and called for greater segregation of the beach from the automobile. He suggested that development instead consist of hiking trails, staircases, and bus service.

Stuart Lefeaux, a UBC grad and park board chairman who later became the university's erosion control manager, was pro-development. He noted that, at the time, "the beach is only approachable for hearty hikers who can navigate one steep trail down 200 feet of cliff."

In 1970 the university hired Swan Wooster to construct a sand-and-gravel berm on the beach. A berm is basically a barrier; its components can vary widely. Eleven years later the *Province* described one such beach berm as "sills of heavy rock filled with gravel placed in front of a 16-metre ... wide sandy strip planted with dune grass." The Wreck berm was specifically designed to slow erosion of the toe of the cliffs. The theory was that the waves would break against the berm rather than eating away the cliffs' sandy base. By the time waves reached the base, much of the water's destructive energy would be dispersed.

As far as protesters were concerned, the issue was that rock and gravel don't make for pretty or comfortable beaches. They basically destroy the beach's natural character in order to preserve it. It's also debatable how much the dumping of such material prevents erosion.

In January 1971, another threat to the beach in its natural state became public. Residents of Point Grey whose homes were threatened by a new road to Locarno and Jericho beaches said publicly that the city was interested in building the road to facilitate a future ferry terminal at Wreck Beach. The road would funnel ferry users to the end of the peninsula. Vancouver mayor Tom Campbell declared that a Wreck terminal would be built "over my dead body." (He did, however, favour a marina at the beach.)

In December 1972, a second erosion-control scheme under discussion was derided by beach user Robert Hamilton in the *Straight*. "I cannot help but wonder if some of [the park board's]

UBC students carved initials into the cliffs throughout the 1970s.
PHILIP TIMMS PHOTO / VANCOUVER PUBLIC LIBRARY 19117

most zealous members as well as certain other local officials do not in fact welcome the loss of the beach. If this beach disappears, so do the bathers, and as a good 80% of the bathers are nasty nudists, what better way to quietly rid themselves of this touchy and embarrassing social and legal problem without having to take some direct concrete action . . . ?" Hamilton made the same claim against another anti-erosion scheme in 1979.

Well aware that opposition would spring up against any proposed beach-development project, UBC's allies made sporadic attempts at public consultation. In 1973, UBC's Alumni Association, housed in the Cecil Green mansion, and the Vancouver park board sponsored an ad in the *Province* that assured the public: "We're building a beach for you." "The beach erosion control project will protect valuable public university buildings which are now threatened," it added, getting to the point.

At a contentious public meeting, attended by a crowd of 200 and reported in the *Ubyssey* of September 27, Swan Wooster presented details of this plan, which was backed by the park board and UBC. It consisted of bolstering the cliffs above Tower Beach with stone groins at 100-metre intervals and reengineering the beach itself with a pebble bed over sand. The issue of nudity was raised for only as long as it took the park board chair to deny that he had any problem with it.

In March 1974, protesters blocked a bulldozer and front-end loader brought in to start the work. Their blockade lasted a full month, until the park board obtained an injunction against them. The protesters, backed by the Sierra Club, appealed but lost. In August, the *Vancouver Sun* reported a seasoned geologist's claim that the project had "completely failed in its purpose . . . [and] may even be aggravating the problem it seeks to solve." A *Sun* headline in 1975 declared the erosion-control measures a "wash-out," but it was another four years before Swan Wooster admitted the winter storms of 1974–75 had partially destroyed the berm.

By 1976 the ongoing erosion battles were so well known that Stan Persky offhandedly mentioned them in his story "The Naked Boy": "Each year at the university a debate about the cliffs raged for a few weeks in the pages of the student paper with ponderous statements by engineers who outdid each other in producing harebrained and expensive erosion-preventing schemes that the students predicted would fail and which inevitably did."

It was also in 1976 that architect Arthur Erickson's showpiece Museum of Anthropology was constructed near the Cecil Green mansion, on the bluffs above Trail Four where a Musqueam warrior's fort had once stood. "We are completely satisfied," Erickson said in 1973, "that there is absolutely no danger to the museum from any future erosion." The design of what was originally known as the Museum of Man included an outdoor reflecting pool, the architect's symbolic recognition of the First Nations heritage that informs the site. After the building was completed, the pool remained unfilled because of worries that, in the event of an earthquake, pool water would cascade over the cliffs and cause further erosion. In 1982, an employee of Arthur Erickson Architects said that filling the pool was "vital" to the building's intended design. It remains empty to this day.

Les Lavkulich and his soil science colleagues were "shocked" — his word — at the site the university chose for the museum. "Up until the 1980s, I don't think the university cared," Lavkulich muses today. "Engineers advised them [of the drawbacks of the proposed site] and the university said it's not a problem, keep developing."

"You don't have to be an environmentalist to know that was a stupid thing to do, to build the museum on the edge of a cliff," remarked Sierra Club chair Rosemary Fox in 1979. "I think it's amazing that an academic institution . . . could have made such an irrational decision."

Swan Wooster Engineering estimated that same year that the building would be safe for a full century, even if cliff erosion continued unchecked. In 1988, UBC's manager of campus planning and development took a different view. Speaking in support of modifications to the cliffs, the manager memorably described the museum as "a million-dollar view behind a $10 fence."

The land between the museum and the beach has always been

By 1968, erosion had almost entirely denuded some slopes above Tower Beach.
UBC ARCHIVES 11589-1

contentious. In 1989 the university cleared blackberry bushes from the area and planted willows without announcing its plans beforehand. At the time, it wasn't clear whether the university even had jurisdiction over the land in question. In March 2006 the university cut down a bunch of trees in the same area, again without previously notifying the GVRD, which manages the cliffs. James Loewen, who went out to survey the damage with Judy Williams afterwards, says they stopped counting downed trees when they reached a hundred. University officials later blamed overzealous staff and said the cutting was a mistake.

UBC had just finished building the Museum of Man when Williams noticed a surveying crew marking trees on the bluffs above the beach. She contacted UBC to find out what was going on. Someone from the university told her not to worry; the surveyors were forestry students. In fact, according to Williams, they were employees of Swan Wooster Engineering, taking measurements for yet another assault on cliff erosion.

"They lied," she says today, still incredulous.

Williams rounded up a committee of "Citizens Concerned for Wreck" and wrote to the newspaper asking why bulldozers had appeared on the beach to clear it of logs and spread more sand fill. "I came out swinging that January," Williams told Natalie Hemsing, who wrote a UBC master's thesis on the subject of place at Wreck Beach in 2005. "Actually I showed up on the beach with a carpenter's apron on and all these tools to dismantle bulldozers. I figured I would do that before I went off to teach school. Who would have thought they would be there at 6:30 in the morning but they were there working. So I never had a chance ... By the time I got to the bottom ... they had already started with bulldozers and had huge mountains of logs crushed. It was just horrible. I was shrieking and crazed. I just flew at them and I wanted to know who was behind it ... I was muddy and dishevelled and full of tears and pissed off at the whole world because our precious beach was being raped like that.

"I caused a three-car pileup sneaking out of school that day. I sneaked out of school five minutes early to try and go to get an injunction. Needless to say I didn't get the injunction ... But then we signed press releases and got the word out and everyone — the Sierra Club and everyone was like, what are you doing? Where is the public input? Well there wasn't any public input because it was just a good old boys' decision. Absolutely horrendous ... piling all that contaminated dredgate up there and they had no environmental monitoring whatsoever."

In 1979, UBC's board of governors appointed a one-man committee, Stanley Weston, to canvass the options and recommend yet another set of erosion-control efforts. An article in the *Ubyssey* questioned his fitness for the job. "I have a lack of confidence in Mr. Weston as far as his dealing with a land-ocean issue," said soil sciences professor Jan Devries. In the same article, Point Grey NDP Association vice-president Bruce Ralston brought up Weston's previous conduct in a land-use study in Langley. According to Ralston, newspaper reports suggested Weston had allowed Gloucester Properties to influence the supposedly independent study findings. Ralston said that Weston's credibility was potentially endangered. Another soil science professor, Art Bomke, said Weston's action in Langley "looks rather fishy."

The university's vice-president, mindful of the ire of Williams and her ilk, promised "full public discussion of the plan by beach users." Weston heard from students, university groups, and the Wreck Beach Committee, as the Preservation Society was then known. In August, the *Vancouver Sun* obtained an unsigned interim report that proposed a bike path be built above Wreck Beach and the cliffs be rounded into gentle slopes. Though the report didn't mention it, these measures would both increase public access and allow the beach to be seen from above, decreasing users' privacy and arguably putting a stop to naked bathing.

Denis Gray-Grant, publisher of the *Western News*, a West Side community paper, speculated on the university's unspoken motivation: "Perhaps the lifestyle down there bothers them." A member of the Scientific Pollution and Environmental Control Society agreed: "There are some underlying political reasons why they want to do this."

On the contrary, according to the university. "There is no intention of ending nude sunbathing," declared Chuck Connaghan, UBC vice-president of administrative services, on August 28. He didn't convince everyone. In a September 12 letter to the *Province*, Robert Hamilton once again claimed erosion-control measures were simply a pretext for ruining the beach for nudists and thus getting rid of them.

Weston officially submitted his report in December 1979. It called for low-impact erosion-control measures, such as construction of a berm like that described by the *Province* in 1981 as "sills of heavy rock filled with gravel." The Wreck Beach Committee recruited Seattle beach expert Wolf Bauer to design the barrier, but later charged that Swan Wooster, recruited once again to install the berm, had modified the original plans beyond recognition.

It probably made little difference. Soil scientist Les Lavkulich says that such measures "are all aspirins. You're treating symptoms, not causes."

In 1983, Korky Day, who had been part of the original Free Beach Defence Fund, was temporarily turfed from the Wreck Beach Committee. There were several cited causes, but Day suspects the real reason was his attempt to turn that year's Walk for Peace nude without first asking the committee. A photo of Day naked, perched atop a billboard catwalk, ran in the *Vancouver Sun*. Since Day refused to shield his genitals, the paper had to airbrush them out.

Day's "Nude Wave" flyer addressed the issue of nudity's relationship to peace in a call to activists to doff their duds. "Some may think we'll distract from the peace movement with a scandalous, cheap, irrelevant gimmick. But we proclaim that nude rights are necessary for lasting peace," he wrote. Judy Williams sent her own letter to the papers, denying any connection between Wreck Beach organizers and Day and Marilyn Hogan's Nudepeace Society.

"It's not the first time or the last time I've been kicked out of an organization and let back in later. I'm just that kind of a guy," Day says brightly. "Fun to kick out, fun to let back in."

By 1985 the Preservation Society had designed membership cards for, as a sample proclaimed, "concerned citizens working to preserve the beach in as nearly natural a state as possible." That included safe water. Fecal coliform counts at Wreck were unacceptably high in places that year and the next, although under 200 (the safety threshold) in most spots. Judy Williams and the society fought for years to have the water tested regularly and the results posted publicly. Because Wreck Beach was not a city beach, it had fewer checks and balances than, say, English Bay downtown or Kits Beach, on the west side of the Point Grey peninsula.

Wreck Beach is only a few kilometres from the sewage outfall at
Iona Park in north Richmond, and unsafe-for-swimming warnings
are still posted occasionally. In the summer of 2006, for example,
bathers were warned not to go into the Fraser River below Trail
Seven, where the Oasis is located. The warning was somewhat
superfluous: most people don't swim in the Fraser anyhow.

The issue of a road reared its head every few years. Police, emergency services, park board employees, or the marina-bent university would argue that it was necessary for access. They would point
out the comparative ease of getting to your boat (at the new marina
that would be built, coincidentally, around the same time), emp-
tying trash cans, arresting the inebriated, and evacuating heart
attack victims if there were a thoroughfare directly to the spot.
Sometimes they mentioned the trials of the handicapped, even if
no actual handicapped person could be found to complain. (Artist
Lenore Herb, herself disabled, has since pushed for and won better TransLink shuttle-bus access to the top of the trails on Marine
Drive.) Stuart Lefeaux, a park board chairman in the 1970s, once
described a beach with no car access as "alienated." But another
chairman, Art Cowie, had assured users as far back as 1973 that
there would "never be a road built on the beach." Users like Korky
Day, in an undated press release, charged the board with ulterior

*Korky Day
was an
enthusiastic
advocate
for 'Nude
Peace'.* BILL
KEAY PHOTO /
PACIFIC PRESS
ARCHIVES

motives: "When you carefully look at the reasons for pushing a road, you realize that those people are merely trying to roust the nudists without looking moralistic."

In 1985 the RCMP requested an access road down to the beach. In response, Judy Williams presented a 12,000-signature anti-road petition to city council, and the park board turned the police down. Still, the increased cost of providing services to a road-free beach clearly rankled some city politicians. "I don't think the citizens of Vancouver would be willing to spend a lot of money on a beach that's the private enclave of an individual lifestyle," remarked right-wing councillor Helen Boyce. Judy Williams quoted Boyce more baldly in the *Wreck Beach News:* "Wreck Beach is a nudist colony funded by the public purse, but the public has no say over it!"

In 1988, a consortium put forward a proposal to barge jet fuel from Washington State to Macdonald Slough, just up the Fraser River from Wreck Beach. Environmentalists claimed the spill threat was unacceptably high, and the plan went no farther.

Two years later, "Wreck's cliffs and trees [were] threatened by David Lam viewing platform," claimed the *Wreck Beach News.* The UBC Botanical Garden, located above Trail Seven, went ahead and built a new viewing area on its grounds, ignoring the society's protests. According to David C. Lam Asian Garden curator Peter Wharton, the lookout was meant to offer visitors a vista over the Strait of Georgia to Vancouver Island, not down onto the gay area of Wreck Beach. The Preservation Society's complaints were "of no consequence," according to the curator. "We realized that they [did] not have any property rights or ownership of the area." He characterizes any fuss as "political squabbling. It really should be in the schoolyard." The GVRD was contracted to do the minimal tree-cutting required to enhance the viewpoint.

In October 1991, Judy Williams accused the university's administration of wishing to permanently alter the beach. "Their long range plans will never happen if WBPS can help it. We fear long term seawall extensions, a roadbed, top-to-toe student condominiums, cliff-shaving, forest removal … and so on." David Grigg, manager of UBC's engineering services, admitted that year that Wreck was "a highly political area."

Williams was not shy about expressing her opinion of the university. In a WBPS newsletter in 1992 she called UBC an "arrogant little kingdom," and two years later she referred to it as the "old arch enemy of Wreck Beach." A 2000 WBPS press release describes UBC as "an institution used to the expediency of a 'little dictator-ship' style of decision-making."

In the latter half of the 1990s, the university embarked on an ambitious program of construction: not the classrooms, dorms, or offices that you'd expect, but private, market-rate residences. The success of the first such development, Hampton Place, was unprecedented. Apparently enough people wanted to live at the end of the peninsula to make more construction commercially viable. By 2006, the cost of two-bedroom apartments in Hampton Place had outpaced even the citywide inflation of real estate: they were now selling for prices in excess of half a million dollars.

Those first buildings also inspired what Dennis Pavlich, uni-versity vice-president of external affairs, characterizes as "enor-mous complaints." Al Poettker, CEO of the UBC Properties Trust, which administers campus building, admits that "people would say, 'You've ruined my neighbourhood, you're destroying my view, you're overpopulating the campus, putting too much traffic on the streets.' There was lots of that." Larry Campbell, former mayor of Vancouver, is one of those who is sharply critical. "If this was all buildings for students, I'd be quite happy with it. But this is an unelected group of people building a city within a city without paying for the resources they use."

As far back as November 1970, a *Ubyssey* editorial about a planned hotel on campus included a prescient description of the later development: "We can have a supermarket on the top floor of the library, a penny arcade along Main Mall or even a Ralph Wil-liams car dealership in C lot. [Williams was famous for a series of hokey television ads, featuring a German shepherd, that promoted his chain of car dealerships.] Maybe we can sell the whole place for 'Academic Acres' subdivision [sic], then start all over again somewhere else."

The penny arcade on Main Mall has morphed into a spanking new Shopper's Drug Mart on University Boulevard, and a faux British-style pub was deemed more useful than a car dealership, but the ambiance of University Town, as it's now called, is oddly reminiscent of the development foreseen in the 1970 editorial.

The actual construction was handed off to arm's-length managers with links to the university's board. The UBC Properties Trust, which was created to administer this process, is a spinoff from the university with one goal: line UBC's coffers. It's in charge of coordinating development on campus, mostly by recruiting market-rate developers to build and sell large condominium complexes to the public. That exclusive focus has left the Trust virtually unfettered. For example, it wasn't originally directed to nudge contractors to employ the sort of green building practices that cost slightly more and take a bit longer than conventional construction methods. (In June 2006, UBC belatedly adopted a building sustainability initiative known as the Residential Environmental Assessment Program.) Nor has the Trust been directed to tap faculty expertise in building, design, or sustainable community planning, even though internationally recognized professors — such as William Rees, who developed the concept of the ecological footprint — are based at UBC. Rees says his students at UBC's School of Planning produced alternative plans for campus development, which they have presented at public meetings, but to no avail. Rees is careful, however, not to single out the university. "The whole idea to me is that UBC is on the leading edge of sustainability, and yet in many respects it's a multi-headed hydra. The corporate side of UBC is out there acting like any other corporate interest, which is to maximize profits within the law. We're moving in all the wrong directions, and UBC is no different from the rest of society in moving in the wrong direction."

Although there are plenty of mixed-use housing goals in the official community plan — the guidelines for building on campus established by UBC and the GVRD in 1991 — they seem notably absent in practice. (According to James Loewen, Dennis Pavlich once told him in a meeting: "That's just a guideline. That's not legally binding.") A co-development scheme that allows groups of faculty to buy campus housing at a potential 20-percent discount, for instance, attracted only one set of participants in each of its first and second years of operation. Even with the discount, the housing is priced close enough to market rates that it is out of reach of most university employees.

The Properties Trust publishes a glossy brochure that explains its position within UBC, details its origins, and describes some of its projects. It doesn't mention the four new student residence towers that the university approved in 2004, to be built just inland from Marine Drive. According to the WBPS, vibrations from construction threaten the cliff faces. (Three subsequent slides in the area below the first tower, Phase One, seem to confirm this fear.) More importantly, the towers, which were designed to be twenty stories high, would be visible from the beach, and beach users would be visible to students in the upper levels of the towers.

Throughout 2005, society members cranked up a campaign against the towers. They sent press releases, urged regulars to write and send letters defending the view from the beach, and circulated a petition against the planned towers. WBPS members attended as many meetings of the university's board of governors, the UBC/GVRD joint committee, and the GVRD as they could. Up to this time, joint committee meetings had always been at the same hour and in the same location. Now, "like clockwork, they would be changed at the last possible moment," recalls WBPS vice-chair James Loewen. In June, the Preservation Society's lawyer Lara Tessaro charged the university with inadequate public consultation, stating that there had only been one thirty-minute public meeting that January to solicit views on the towers. Dennis Pavlich quibbled; the single meeting, he said, had lasted almost two hours.

The WBPS intensified its publicity campaign, inviting reporters to come out to the beach to see a blimp hovering at the height of the as-yet-unbuilt first tower to show how far the building would rise above the treeline behind the beach. The university contested the beachers' estimate of the height and raised its own balloon. WBPS members toted photomontages of the projected towers looming over the beach to GVRD board meetings. They made impassioned speeches to city councillors about the sanctity of the natural viewscape. UBC fought back, contending that an agreement with the GVRD not to have buildings visible from the beach applied only to the strip of sand left at high tide. Eventually the first tower, now built, was capped at eighteen stories. The original fifty-seven–metre height would have exceeded the university's own official community plan building guidelines by four metres.

"We are extremely skeptical about UBC's willingness to actually incorporate public feedback and input into its design," society members stated in a press release on October 3, 2005. "Just one

The Wreck Beach Preservation Society's mockup, and actual tower above the treeline.

JAMES LOEWEN PHOTO

day after the public hearing on October 5th, UBC plans to send its current proposal for Phase Two to its Advisory Urban Design Panel (AUDP) for approval, despite our understanding that the public will have until the end of October to provide feedback."

"Since 1974, the Wreck Beach Preservation Society (WBPS) has called for public input *before, not after* the fact," Judy Williams commented pointedly in a letter to the *Vancouver Courier* that same year.

Les Lavkulich is not surprised by the furor. He has been a professor since 1968, and in his experience, the university goes through phases. There's the old-school view — "We'll do it and tell you what we've done." There's the twentieth-century view — "We'll get a committee and consult with some stakeholders, but we decide who those stakeholders are." Lavkulich doesn't get to the third stage; he doesn't have to say that UBC hasn't either. "Dennis," he says of the university's vice-president of external affairs, "is the twentieth century."

Larry Campbell agrees. He sat on GVRD meetings when he was mayor of Vancouver. Today he characterizes UBC's administrative attitude as "We're going to build it and we don't care what they say."

Officials at the university and at the Properties Trust feel the same sense of frustration as members of the Preservation Society, albeit in reverse. "We made lots of gestures. Significant substantive gestures," says Al Poettker, president and CEO of the Trust. "And we never got credit for them. On the contrary. There was on [the WBPS] website, 'Look what we've accomplished so far.'" He discounts the society's anti-tower petition, which eventually gathered more than 47,000 signatures. "Municipalities pay scant attention to petitions," he says dismissively. "[People will] sign just so you'll go away. We had affidavits from people who say they were harassed to sign the petition."

Trust employees have gone so far as to deny the beach's history. "Wreck Beach didn't exist," Jas Sahota, a project manager, tells me outside Al Poettker's office late one afternoon. He's presumably referring to the era before 1977, when the dredgate that makes up the beach's present contours was dumped, but the comment could also be taken as a larger philosophical statement.

Paul Young, the Trust's director of planning and design, is less categorical. He is the only high-ranking Trust employee to visit Wreck Beach on a regular basis and is thus uniquely positioned to understand both parties' points of view. "It's always easy to get someone to sign a petition against development, no matter where it is. It's very easy for UBC to be painted as the bad guy." He pauses and admits, "UBC does tend to be quite conservative. The hardcore users tend to be ..." Young searches for a word, "the other way.

"If we'd known the problems, we probably would have considered a different building shape," Young says of the towers. Still, he thinks the fuss is all out of proportion. "Many people were misled as to the extent of the visibility of the towers from the beach. I would have signed a petition," he confesses, engagingly. "I would have been offended as to what they [the Preservation Society] were showing was going to happen." Then again, Young is not anti-development. "I wouldn't mind sitting on the beach and being able to see a building."

Soon he'll be able to see not one, but several. The university appears to have won the fight, with the towers — three now instead of four, with two smaller seven-story buildings alongside and the towers' maximum height capped at eighteen stories — scheduled to be finished by 2008.

These days, Judy Williams festoons her car with bumper stickers declaring "Shame on UBC: Put Your Towers Where the Sun Doesn't Shine." She also hands out the stickers to supporters. "We're an embarrassment," Williams declares flatly, dismissing UBC's attitude as one of "body shame." Society members joke about the university, but the jokes have a bitter tinge. Regular Marilyn Hogan remembers a spoof slogan designed by a student at the university: "UBC Inc.: Building Community Whether You

Want It or Not." Hogan wishes the slogan would be fashioned into a T-shirt. "I'd wear it."

Rightly or wrongly, WBPS members see UBC administrators as unaware of and uninterested in the treasure under their noses. As Al Poettker says, "UBC has always been known and defined by its landscape, but you can have too much of a good thing."

The beach "celebrates freedom — sexual freedom, emotional freedom," says James Loewen. "It's the antithesis of what the university thinks it should be. It's sad to have something so precious, as Vancouver grows, for UBC not to have the insight to see the value of that."

On both sides, the conflict has grown almost intimate. "Utterly neurotic," snaps Dennis Pavlich of what he calls, with deliberate impersonality, the Preservation Society's "leadership." He illustrates this categorization with a story about a meeting at which he referred to beachgoers as "unorthodox." Afterwards, he says, Judy Williams approached him and said, "'So you do think it's unorthodox.' As if," he says now, "thinking it was unorthodox was a problem in itself." But Pavlich doesn't want anyone to get the wrong impression. "I love them all, so there you are."

Hogan, a soft-spoken blonde woman sometimes mistaken by the uninitiated for Judy Williams, had a dream one night in the middle of the tower fight. She was down on Wreck Beach, and so were Dennis Pavlich and Al Poettker. The two men were naked, sitting in a log house, and playing backgammon. Poettker glanced up to remark that he needed a cold one. "Now you know what all the fuss is about," Hogan remembers thinking. Alas, it was only a dream.

Mitch Sokalski can see both sides of the question. Of the GVRD's comparative willingness to listen to beach supporters, he says simply, "We're a public agency. They're not." He adds of UBC, "They love the park. They love the foreshore. And they love the university more. What's wrong with that?"

"They just wanted to win and be done with it," says Korky Day of the towers' planners. "So did we."

"My major concern at the moment," says soil scientist Les Lavkulich, "is the development on campus is now about 3,000 times faster than it was in the 1980s. When you cover over everything by concrete ... cities flood. We know there's been erosion

[on the cliffs]; we know activity hastens that erosion. [The towers] can be the tipping point. We don't know. We do know it's cumulative. Engineers are site specific," he points out, meaning that they look only at the building site, not at the cumulative result for campus or construction's eventual impact on cliffsides. "There's a connection between intensity of rainfall, infiltration, and surface runoff. [The result of this] won't show for quite a few years. There's a timeframe that people are unaware of. Eventually [the peninsula] will dry out."

Dennis Pavlich stands in front of construction at the university. PAUL JOSEPH PHOTO

Lavkulich's recommendation? "We need to try to mimic nature in terms of its hydrological routine." Halting, reversing, or at least mitigating the pace of development by deploying surfaces other than concrete or glass would allow water to trickle naturally through the aquifer instead of becoming concentrated in storm sewers and further ravaging cliffsides.

Behind beachgoers' anger at UBC's construction imperatives is a real sense of loss. The view from the beach, with buildings hidden by the cliffs, has always been celebrated. Back in 1972, Al Anderson wrote in the radical paper the *Grape* that Wreck Beach "begins just at the point where the view of the city across English Bay gets mercifully blotted out by a shoulder of woodland."

"Until the first tower was completed in 2005," Marilyn Hogan confirms in an e-mail, "when you ambled out at low tide to gaze back at the trees on the bluff, that was the best vantage to drink in the view and experience the sense of timelessness it offered and the feeling of being miles away from the civilization. Now it's still lovely of course — until you get out far enough to see the first tower. Then the bubble is burst and you are once again reminded of the mundane reality of inanimate structures."

James Loewen concurs. "Previous to these towers, the beach below was unspoiled. It was an area that people came to from around the world," he told a *Province* reporter in February 2006. "It was incredible you could be so close to the city, and yet feel so removed from it. Now, with the visual intrusion of these towers, this is compromised to a great degree."

Although he doesn't think of the towers themselves as a problem, Paul Young believes that the new residents construction brings to campus might be. "Once there's more people, the pressure is for Wreck culture to change. It's kind of like a piece of the counterculture from the sixties that's living on. You only see that at Wreck Beach now."

FIVE

Tomorrow's Beach

The year starts early at Wreck Beach. January 1 is the date of the annual Polar Bear Swim. Judy Williams has participated for more than three decades. "Of course I had to get snookered first to do it," she says at an après-dunk party on the first day of 2006.

The Polar Bear Swim was when newly minted constable Robert Ploughman first saw Wreck Beach. He was "scared to death," he says now, but that had nothing to do with his destination. "All new Mounties are scared to death." Beachgoers, in time-honoured tradition, had built bonfires on the beach to warm themselves after their dip. His new partner, who was showing him around, wasn't much more experienced than Ploughman himself. She freaked — open fires were prohibited — and ordered regulars to extinguish them. Ploughman saw first-hand the results of a strict adherence to the rules: "They got angry and tried to run us off the beach."

By February of a mild year, diehard beachers are already ensconced in an area north of the main beach called the Condos (not to be confused with the little spots colonized by regulars on the gayside). Up a slope, around the corner from Trail Six and heading towards Four, the Condos are a wide, sandy shelf three metres above the beach proper. With the right combination of sun reflectors, regulars say, it is possible to sunbathe nude there on a calm, early spring day.

As for the gayside, "about twenty of us will go in the wintertime. It's probably one of the warmest spots" on the beach, says Rick Fearman. "Any time from October to March. If the forecast is nice, it's surprising how many fellows will come out for a walk."

*The Condos, just north of the current main beach before the point,
consist of a wide, sandy shelf partway up the cliffs. Regulars say it
is possible to sunbathe there even in February. The flower gardens
are planted and maintained by regulars.* DON SLADE PHOTO

There is no calm spot at the foot of Trail Four in February or
March. Even a sunny afternoon finds the sea roiling and angry-
looking, useful only for staring at in wistful contemplation and,
preferably, solitude. Above the beach, near the Museum of
Anthropology, the susurration of wind in the trees combined with
the crash of waves below is deafening, like a helicopter taking off.

Early-bird students eking out an advance taste of summer come
down to the beach in April, mainly so they can go back to their
dorms afterwards to write bragging e-mails to those in unluckier
regions of the country. Wreck's larger population of summer visitors doesn't begin to trickle back until later in April, May, or even
June, depending on the weather. On a cloudy day in the middle
of June, the beach is more like someone's backyard than a public
place. Low conversations float from house to house, with everyone
glancing up at the sky to see what's developing. A swirl of cloud,
a few scattered drops, then sun again — undecided weather. The
vendors are few and far between: the looming Nordic guy, some-

one else proffering Jell-O shooters. As the day heats up, mist lifts off the surface of the tide pools. It drifts across the disappearing sands, preceding the tide.

Most people don't find it warm enough to swim in the ocean until midsummer. That's when the city becomes hot enough that Wreck Beach beckons, oasis-like, from the end of the peninsula. July and August are carnival months. "Life is a slice when you taste my pizza, but life is more fun when you taste my bun," remarks the itinerant vendor of Chinese BBQ buns and Hawaiian pies in insulated sacks. The beach is a carpet of flesh, bared and in various states of dress. Starting at five o'clock most weekdays, there's an unofficial shift change. Daytimers trickling home for dinner pass newly freed office workers streaming down the stairs, their suit jackets off and dress shirts open at the neck. Back on the sands, the police patrols are out in force, picking their way among the bodies in their full navy uniforms. Everyone is here, including the nude lawyer who jumps up, impromptu, to advise the arrested on their rights.

Midsummer is also when official beach holidays are scheduled, from Wreck Beach Day, with its kite-flying, sandcastle, and body-painting competitions, to the Pacific Canadian Association of Nudists' annual gayside picnic and the August Bare Buns Run, which is one of three such runs (the other two take place at nude resorts in Washington State). The Kokoro Dance Theatre troupe performs here one weekend in July, its butoh dancers painted a ghostly white as they writhe on the sands.

September is a gradual slide from the heat of August, with the sands still full of beachgoers delaying the inevitable, but October is far from the furor of summer. It's cool enough that people bundle into multiple layers, but the diehards are still on the beach, standing now, drinking their eternal cans of beer. A last vendor wanders by — "Chilled beverages" — like an afterthought, and a couple of collectors. They mash the empty cans against the logs before storing them in their sacks. The vendor is hailed, interrogated. He can't, a customer remarks, be getting much business. He concurs, but shrugs that it's "something to do." They make the exchange: a Kokanee for two toonies. It's the circle of life, Wreck-style.

Dogs are allowed out of season, and they are here in variety: a collie streaking after a ball, an alert chocolate Doberman pacing the sand, a giant black Lab named Bubba wading in the surf. After a while the collie stops and, sitting down, gazes at the sunset.

The sand darkens and turns steely grey as the sun shortens its blazing trail across the water. The squared-off grids of houses are empty, a temporarily abandoned city. Out there, in the blue, ships pass: a fishing boat with its angled upright gear, a Zodiac that turns and makes its way in to shore. The inflatable pulls up, and several people who have built a crackling, smoke-puffing bonfire hail the new arrival.

Winter settles in, gloomy and thick. Various groups hold nude nights at Vancouver-area pools to tide beachers over — the mandated lifeguards, in case you're wondering, wear clothes — but the swimmers are only marking time until next year. If there's a facsimile of summer's warm heat to be had in a chlorinated tub, nobody's found it yet.

December brings Watermelon's annual Wreck Beach Preservation Society fundraiser. It's a sprawling affair with silent auction, special cocktails, and the biggest concentration of beachers to be found outside of the warmer months. The beach's most famous vendor serves cocktails and wears a typically fetching outfit: one year, it was a Kelly green vintage frock and long red wig. Women in evening gowns or white yoga pants paired with stilettos bob on the dance floor. A Frenchman pauses outside on the steps to the front door. Below him the smokers are clustered on the sidewalk, but the weed they're puffing isn't tobacco. "The women look so good here!" he confides unprompted to a bystander. "On the beach, you see them naked and you think, *pfui*, nothing. But with makeup, and their hair done, and clothes on . . ."

In the most beautiful city on earth, new threats to the beach can come from anywhere. In the spring of 2006, planners overseeing construction of a new rapid-transit line to Richmond had a bright idea. Why not use the fill from tunnelling to form an artificial island off Wreck Beach? Judy Williams derided the proposal as "Orwellian."

Looming on the beach's horizon is the question of the Fraser River debris trap. The trap, which most people have never even heard of, is located upriver at Hope, 154 kilometres east of Vancouver, and removes wood debris from the river each year during spring runoff. If the debris were collected in one place, it would form a pile as high as a thirteen-story building and as long as a football field. The trap is funded by a patchwork of sources: federal, provincial, regional, and municipal governments and the private sector (mainly the logging industry). Since there is no long-term guarantee for funding, there is a scramble each year to ensure there is enough money to continue operations. Judy Williams keeps a watchful eye on the issue, aware of the problems that debris would cause downriver at Wreck Beach. Such matters may not grab the headlines, but they are Williams's forte. "I don't have a husband, I don't have kids. This is my life," she says of the beach.

Regulars, past and present, are aware of how much they owe her. "There wouldn't be a Wreck Beach without Judy Williams. She is totally 150 percent for the beach," says Donna Watts. "She's a bulldozer. You needed a bulldozer."

Watermelon goes further. "We're pleasure seekers," she says of herself and other Wreck Beach regulars. "And Judy does the work that makes it possible for us to have our pleasure."

Williams herself has summed up how she feels about Wreck. "It

The unglamorous Fraser River debris trap, 154 km upriver from Wreck: 'Without it, you wouldn't have a beach,' says Marion Robinson of the Fraser Basin Council. PHOTO COURTESY FRASER BASIN COUNCIL

Kids have always been a feature of Wreck Beach, like these tots constructing sand castles under Trail Four in the 1970s. DON SLADE PHOTO

must be remembered that it is a people's beach, of the people, for the people, by the people."

"I consider Wreck Beach to be more than a curiosity," says Don Rosenbloom, the lawyer who defended Wreck-goers arrested for indecent exposure in 1970. "I consider it to be part of our mosaic. I consider it to be part of our city and of our lifestyle. It's certainly part of our history, and it's a statement of the tolerance that is exhibited in the city. It's an incredible story that within a city of two million people, within a hop, skip, and a jump of downtown Vancouver, on a beautiful day, you can have two or three thousand people nude on a beach. That's something to celebrate. Doesn't that say something about our lifestyle? What distinguishes us from every Tom, Dick, and Harry city? Well, this is one of those things."

"Where else do you have 5,000 people on a busy Saturday on an isolated beach and I was able to keep the peace by myself with only a young summer Constable for backup!" exclaims Robert Ploughman in an e-mail.

"It's a place so alive and full of stunning surprises you'd think it was bewitched," wrote Al Anderson in 1972.

The future of Wreck Beach remains, as always, precarious. Every few months now, there is a memorial for another beacher.

The obituaries in the WBPS's newsletters are lengthy and personal: "One of his beach friends, Shirley R., left repeated messages for him to call her after she had dreamed he was in trouble. Finally, Aug. 20, she insisted that the caretaker of Shane's apartment let her in."

The regulars tend to stick together. Marilyn Hogan thinks the word "community" is not amiss. "I think we have that pretty strongly at Wreck Beach ... A guy who was ill got a car when he needed one," she muses, adding that she knows "four or five hundred" regulars by sight, if not by name.

Don Slade, the photographer who documented Wreck extensively in the 1970s, thinks 2005 was his last year on the beach. He can't manage the stairs anymore, and it takes him hours to walk around from the Spanish Banks foreshore. As they age, regulars can still go to Acadia Beach, with its relatively gentle slopes. It is technically part of Wreck, but nobody pretends it's the same.

James Loewen, WBPS vice-chair, remembers his own initial, timid, clothed forays as a teenager. Perhaps that is why he thinks that no matter what happens to its current core of regulars, the beach will endure. "The spirit of Wreck Beach is all-inclusive," he says. "When you hear those jungle drums at night, it's very persuasive. Places have a way of seeping into your soul, and you become a part of them, and I'd like to think that at least some of those kids will feel that way down the road."

GLOSSARY

Attitude Point   Widened area of shore fed by cliffslide slump in the mid-1990s. It is past the breakwater, in the gay area, about halfway down the path from Trail Six to Trail Seven. Also known as Bitch Beach. More recently referred to as the Oasis.

beerball   Men-only combination of rugby, football, and basketball, in which knocking a can of beer off the pole is the object of the game, and taking the ball from opponents by any means necessary is the strategy. Winner gets the beer.

bucktail   First-time nudist, so called because of the white flash of their never-seen-sun bottom.

Casino   A house where they play cards, dice, and other games of chance; sometimes marked by a giant fuzzy die on a pole.

Condos   A wind-sheltered niche in the cliff, built up by logs, around the north corner from the main beach. This is where wintertime regulars set up solar reflectors to catch the sun. This term can also refer to regulars' driftwood-lined areas on the gay side of the beach. See also **house.**

genital-hiding community   Korky Day's description of the clothed. See also **textiles.**

house   Logged-off section of beach where regulars sit. Named houses include the White House (AKA the Old Folks' Home) and the Casino. They are often landscaped, with improvements/additions (seating, flower gardens, ashtrays, first aid kits).

Jurassic Park   Widening of shoreline on gayside past Trail Seven. This is a small area open to the river where older men gather.

naturist   Sometimes pronounced "nah-turist," this is a 60s-nouveau term for (optionally, back-to-nature) nudist. Naturists are happy to go nude in a public area, such as a beach, as opposed to a private club.

nude Nazis   Wreck Beach regulars who police an area of beach where clothes are not allowed. See also **Old Folks' Home, White House.**

nudist   Old-school term for the unclothed by choice, who are often found at a nudist colony or nudist resort.

Old Folks' Home   Logged-off section of main beach for longtime regulars, complete with gardens, first aid kits, ashtrays, and other conveniences. Also known as the White House.

Pharmacy   The area at the bottom of Trail 6 where hard drugs were once sold.

Pop Tart Beach   The area of beach grass past the breakwater. So called because the boys pop up there. See also **Scary Grass.**

Pop-Up Beach (or Point)   The first grassy shoreline area available for sunning down gayside beach trail. The men pop up from behind logs, like prairie dogs, whenever a newcomer appears.

Scary Grass   The area of beach grass halfway between the main beach and Oasis. So called because you never know what you'll find there. Also known as the flats. See also **Pop Tart Beach.**

Secret Beach   The sheltered, sandy, extreme tip of the break-water, invisible from the shore of the main beach. It can be reached by sand at low tide; otherwise visitors must clamber over breakwater's rocks. Also known as Gilligan's Island.

skimboarding   A sport in which the user tosses a short, fat wooden board so that it skims along the surface of the water, then runs behind and jumps atop, trying to maintain her balance. Usually practised at the water's edge for ease of running and jumping. What to do when you can't snowboard.

skyclad   Neohippie term for nude.

textiles   What nudists call clothed people.

White House   Longtime regulars' logged-off section of beach, also known as the Old Folks' Home.

ACKNOWLEDGEMENTS

My gratitude goes out to all those who so generously shared their memories, impressions, stories, pictures, research, and files on the subject of the beach with me: Brian Baxter, Dennis Bolen, Sandra Boutilier, Larry Campbell, Grace Chan, Korky Day, Rick Fearman, Larry Grant, Natalie Hemsing, Lenore Herb, Marilyn Hogan, Precious Hutchinson, James Loewen, Anne Merling, Dennis Pavlich, Stan Persky, Robert Ploughman, Al Poettker, Don Slade, Mitch Sokalski, Watermelon, Brian and Donna Watts, Peter Wharton, and Paul Young.

But my greatest thanks must go to Judy Williams, without whom Wreck Beach as we know it would be a far lesser place.

C.B.
Vancouver
July 2007

SOURCES AND FURTHER READING

BOOKS, REPORTS, AND ARTICLES

Anderson, Al. "Wreck Beach: Eros and erosion." *The Grape*, August 16–23, 1972.

Arnett, John. "UBC unveils its plans for new Museum of Man." *UBC Reports*, 19:2 (January 18, 1973).

Austin, Edie. "Wreck beach fans want area left in natural state: Environmentalists rap idea of sodded Point Grey cliffs." *Vancouver Sun*, August 22, 1979.

Baxandall, Lee. *World Guide to Nude Beaches and Recreation*. New York: Harmony Publishers, 1981.

Bermingham, John. "GVRD allows highrises to overlook nude beach." Vancouver *Province*, February 19, 2006.

"Berms away!" Vancouver *Province*, April 2, 1981.

Bocking, Michael. "$12 million plan proposed to stop cliff erosion at UBC." *Vancouver Sun*, August 21, 1979.

Chan, Grace. "How WB came to be: The history below the 362 steps down Trail 6." Unpublished manuscript, Vancouver, March 26, 1999.

Cook, Michelle. "Alumni welcome home for Reunion Weekend." *UBC Reports*, 47:14, September 20, 2001.

"Cowie pledged 'no road on beach'." *Vancouver Sun*, September 8, 1973.

Day, Korky. "Wreck beach road plan revived!" Undated press release, circa 1979.

———. "Nude Wave." Undated flyer, circa 1983.

Decker, Jeff. "Can't wreck her beach: A profile of Judy Williams." *N magazine*, March 2006. Available online at www.naturistsociety.com/magazine/list.jsp. Accessed August 2006.

Evans, Rhys. "Paradise on the margins or paradise lost? Tolerance, permissiveness and conflict on Wreck Beach." Arkleton Research Paper No. 5. Aberdeen: Arkleton Centre For Rural Development Research, University of Aberdeen, 2000.

Furstenwald, Maria. "The beach road." *Ubyssey*, October 24, 1969.

Gerard, Bernice. *Bernice Gerard: Today and for Life*. Burlington, ON: Welsh Publishing, 1988.

————. "Average citizen loses in 'nudist takeover'" (letter to the editor). *Vancouver Sun*, July 9, 1977.

Gold, Kerry. "Nudists creeping too close to the clothed." *Vancouver Sun*, April 1, 2006.

Greater Vancouver Regional District. "Official community plan for part of Electoral Area 'A' and GVRD-UBC memorandum of understanding." Vancouver: Author, 1997.

————. Pacific Spirit Regional Park management plan. Vancouver: Author, 1991.

Grindlay, Lora. "Surrey mayor asks nudists to cover up on family beach." Vancouver *Province*, July 25, 2006.

Hainsworth, Jeremy. "Already a legend." *Xtra West*, September 18, 2002.

Hambleton, Ronald. *Every Man Is an Island*. London: Hutchinson, 1957.

Hamilton, Robert. Letter to the editor. Vancouver *Province*, September 12, 1979.

————. "Death of Wreck Beach." *Georgia Straight*, December 21, 1972.

Hamsing, Natalie. "Production of place: Community, conflict and belonging at Wreck Beach." Master's thesis, Department of Anthropology, University of British Columbia, 2005.

Hossie, Linda. "Wreck Beach campers to continue basking in the sun: They blame day-trippers for garbage problems." *Vancouver Sun*, August 7, 1974.

Howell, Mike. "RAV dirt would make good island, says planning chair." *Vancouver Courier*, November 16, 2005.

Kass, Sandy. "Jericho may turn into Vancouver's own Coney Island." *Ubyssey*, January 26, 1971.

————. "Over Tom's dead body." *Ubyssey*, February 2, 1971.

Keating, Jack. "Man whose body washed ashore was murdered." Vancouver *Province*, October 19, 2006.

A Living Working River: An Estuary Management Plan for the Fraser River. Vancouver: Fraser River Estuary Management Program, August 1994.

MacLeod, Pat. "Erosion controlled, UBC gains time." *Ubyssey*, May 12, 1982.

Natural, Mr. [Korky Day]. "Nude in changed to Wreck Beach." *Georgia Straight*, August 19–26, 1970.

Norman, Emma Spenner. "Point Grey pre-university (pre-1890): Coast Salish and industry." In *Recovering the University Fabric*. Vancouver: UBC Archives, n.d. www.library.ubc.ca/archives/u_fabric/pre1890.html. Accessed September 18, 2006.

"One man force taken to task." *Ubyssey*, November 15, 1979.

Persky, Stan. "The Naked Boy." Bed. N.p., n.d. Circa 1976.

Rushton, Doug. "Beach erosion control 'flop.'" *Vancouver Sun*, August 14, 1974.

"UBC will seek public reaction to erosion plan." *UBC Reports*, 25:16 (September 12, 1979).

Volkart, Carol. "Wreck Beach fans fight to save their cliffs." *Vancouver Sun*, August 28, 1979.

"We're building a beach for you" (advertisement). Vancouver *Province*, March 30, 1974.

"What next?" *Ubyssey*, November 6, 1970.

Williams, Judy. "Don't wreck the beach" (letter to the editor). Vancouver *Province*, November 28, 2005.

Wilson, Deborah. "Famous nudists' haven threatened." *Globe and Mail*, September 13, 1990. Reprinted in *Nude & Natural* 10:3.

Woycke, James. *Au Naturel: The History of Nudism in Canada*. Etobicoke, ON: Federation of Canadian Naturists, 2003.

"Wreck Beach: Nudists told not to stray." Vancouver *Province*, March 21, 1978.

NEWSPAPERS

Ubyssey. Various issues, 1955 – present.

Vancouver Courier. September 11, 1985, October 28, 1988.

Province. February 18, 1969; February 27, 1969; March 20, 1973; July 12, 1978; August 26, 1990; February 16, 1994.

Wreck Beach Preservation Society Newsletter. Various issues.

WEBSITES

Wreck Beach Preservation Society: www.wreckbeach.org.

Watermelon: www.melongirl.com

Copyright New Star Books 2007

All rights reserved. No part of this work may be reproduced or used
in any form or by any means — graphic, electronic, or mechani-
cal — without the prior written permission of the publisher. Any
request for photocopying or other reprographic copying must be
sent in writing to ACCESS Copyright.

NEW STAR BOOKS LTD.
107 - 3477 Commercial Street, Vancouver, BC v5N 4E8   CANADA
1574 Gulf Road, No. 1517, Point Roberts, WA 98281   USA
www.NewStarBooks.com   *info@NewStarBooks.com*

TRANSMONTANUS is edited by Terry Glavin. Editorial correspon-
dence should be sent to 3813 Hobbs Street, Victoria, BC v8P 5c8

Edited by Audrey McClellan
Cover by Mutasis.com
Cover photo by Don Slade
Map by Eric Leinberger
Typesetting by New Star Books
Printed & bound in Canada by Gauvin Press, Gatineau, QC
First printing, August 2007
Printed on 100% post-consumer recycled paper

The publisher acknowledges the financial support of the Government of Canada through the Canada Council and the Department
of Canadian Heritage Book Publishing Industry Development Program, and of the Province of British Columbia through the British
Columbia Arts Council and the Book Publishing Tax Credit.

LIBRARY AND ARCHIVES CANADA CATALOGUING IN PUBLICATION

Brooks, Carellin
   Wreck Beach / Carellin Brooks.

(Transmontanus ; 16)
Includes bibliographical references.
ISBN 978-1-55420-031-3

   1. Wreck Beach (Vancouver, B.C.). 2. Nude beaches — British
Columbia — Vancouver. I. Title. II. Series.

GV451.3.C3B76 2007   613'.1940971133   C2007-903908-1